NEOLIBERALISM AND THE VOLUNTARY AND COMMUNITY SECTOR IN NORTHERN IRELAND

Ciaran Hughes and Markus Ketola

First published in Great Britain in 2021 by

Policy Press, an imprint of
Bristol University Press
University of Bristol
1–9 Old Park Hill
Bristol
BS2 8BB
UK
t: +44 (0)117 954 5940
e: bup-info@bristol.ac.uk

Details of international sales and distribution partners are available at:
policy.bristoluniversitypress.co.uk

British Library Cataloguing in Publication Data
A catalogue record for this book is available from the British Library

ISBN 978-1-4473-5118-4 hardcover
ISBN 978-1-4473-5124-5 ePub
ISBN 978-1-4473-5119-1 ePdf

Cover design by Gareth Davies at Qube Design Associates
Front cover image: iStock.com
Printed and bound in Great Britain by CPI Group (UK) Ltd,
Croydon, CR0 4YY
Bristol University Press and Policy Press use environmentally responsible
print partners

Contents

List of abbreviations

CCNI	Charity Commission for Northern Ireland
CDO	community development organisation
CDW	community development worker
EU	European Union
GFA	Good Friday Agreement
NGO	non-governmental organisation
NI	Northern Ireland
NICVA	Northern Ireland Council for Voluntary Action
UK	United Kingdom
VCS	voluntary and community sector

Acknowledgements

We would like to thank academic colleagues from several institutions for their help and advice, and Ulster University for providing invaluable institutional support during the research. We would like to thank the staff at Building Change Trust, and the VCS and public sector staff who took time to discuss the topics explored in this book. Thank you to Laura Vickers-Rendall and the team at Bristol University Press for their patience and advice. Many thanks to our friends and family for all their support and encouragement. Any errors or omissions are ours.

Series editor's foreword

John Mohan

The extent to which greater devolution in the UK has resulted in divergences in the development of voluntary action, and in the roles, resources and responsibilities of voluntary organisations, is a question on which we lack detailed empirical studies. Differences between the devolved administrations in terms of individual behaviours such as volunteering or charitable giving largely disappear, once allowance is made for individual and community characteristics. Comparisons of organisational populations and resources are to a degree occluded by regulatory differences seem more likely to be rooted in economic conditions in communities, rather than policy differences.

Consideration of such indicators only gets us so far, and studies are urgently needed of policy and practice in the voluntary sector in the devolved administrations. The position of civil society in Northern Ireland offers a crucial test case for the claims made for the voluntary sector's contribution to social development. This study by Hughes and Ketola is the first recent book-length treatment of such questions, and constitutes a highly original study of the place of voluntary action in the devolved administrations of the UK.

The voluntary sector in Northern Ireland has become a key agent in post-conflict reconstruction since the Good Friday Agreement of 1998. But the burden of expectations placed upon civil society there was high well before that momentous event. Given the longstanding distrust of state institutions, communities understandably turned to voluntary organisations which, during the period of direct rule from Westminster, played a crucial role in the delivery of social programmes.

From 1998, Northern Ireland experienced what has been described as a 'double transition' towards peace, and towards neoliberalism. While post-conflict reconstruction led to very substantial influxes of funding for voluntary and community organisations, such beneficence was never expected to continue indefinitely. As a consequence, the reality has been one of partnerships between the voluntary sector and government. Hughes and Ketola's study has important insights to offer concerning the rhetoric and reality of partnerships between voluntary organisations and governments, and it also makes a significant contribution to debates about what has been characterised as a generic 'partnership turn' in the sector.

This study is also about a core dilemma facing voluntary and community organisations in the context of neoliberalism, a specific outcome of which is a narrowing of the scope of funding streams. This poses challenges for organisations in terms of their ability to promote social innovation, cooperate, meet community needs, and all the while maintaining their independence. The third sector in Northern Ireland encompasses organisations many of which, owing their origins to sectarian conflict, see their core mission as a radical and provocative one with a commitment to defending particular groups. However, these are in tension with a professionalised sector co-opted into state-determined agendas and benefiting from the massive influx of European funding associated with regeneration and peace building. The comfortable official rhetoric of partnership and cooperation does not therefore correspond easily to the realities of the experiences of this diverse population of individual organisations.

These concerns are redolent of longstanding debates in the wider British voluntary sector about bifurcations between, on the one hand, large professionalised organisations delivering services, and on the other, a radical, less formalised set of organisational entities, operating outwith the narrow confines of discourses focused on managerial efficiency and partnership. Hughes and Ketola thus speak to issues which are at the core of current debates in the field. They point to growing evidence of waning enthusiasm for rhetorics of partnership, and suggest that voluntary organisations need to move away from such formalised relationships towards a rediscovery of the 'creative chaos' that is at the heart of voluntarism.

ONE

Introduction

Policymakers often place rather unrealistic expectations on the shoulders of civil society, including that aspect of civil society that is commonly referred to as the voluntary and community sector (VCS). In policy narratives, the VCS is often described as a facilitator of localised voluntary action that can help address unmet social needs; it is seen to provide a 'voice' for the poor and marginalised, and in the case of Northern Ireland (NI) in particular, the VCS was believed to be a bridge between fragmented communities. In the context of these optimistic accounts of voluntary and community action, the VCS has come to be seen as a key agent in the drive towards a more egalitarian, prosperous and democratic society. The formal organisations that inhabit civil society are also seen as central actors in the delivery of governance reforms that will enable governments to empower communities and make services more responsive to citizen demands, for it is through the VCS that service designers are able to tap into grassroots knowledge and expertise. By working in partnership with civil society, it is claimed, government will deliver services more effectively and efficiently, but it will also make decisions more democratically. But to what extent does the reality match these optimistic narratives?

Answering this question is a central motivation behind this book. By taking a detailed look at the case of NI, we explore the nature and extent of neoliberal policy reforms in the region, the repeated 'partnership turns' in government rhetoric and policy, and the impact this has had on the Northern Irish VCS. As we do so, we draw on a substantial body of empirical research conducted between 2013 and 2019, as well as a review of relevant publications from the UK and NI governments. We explore the narratives that surround and describe the VCS, government–VCS partnerships and network and relationship building. These particular narratives have emerged in the context of post-Good Friday Agreement (GFA) NI, but we will also see that they are reflective of broader policy discourses and trajectories elsewhere in the UK, Europe and beyond.

Structure of the book

In essence, this book concerns the role of the VCS in the neoliberal governance reforms that signalled the 'partnership turn' in government policy. We look at the active role the VCS has taken in rolling out these reforms, and how 'working in partnership' and being 'networked' and 'connected' have come to be understood as important parameters through which the VCS takes stock of itself and articulates its value. In Chapter Two, we begin by charting the 'partnership turn' in UK government policy, from its Conservative Party foundations in the Thatcherite project of promoting voluntarism to the 'third way' of New Labour and through to the 'Big Society' agenda under the more recent Conservative administrations (Macmillan, 2013). The second part of the chapter locates these broader developments within the specific history of community development and voluntary action in NI, particularly in terms of the exceptional role played by the region's VCS during the Troubles and in the wake of the peace process. An understanding of the historical role and nature of the VCS in the region is important for explaining the VCS's reconfigured role and nature in light of more recent governance reforms and NI's 'double transition' to peace and neoliberalism (McCabe, 2013, 4).

The three chapters that follow constitute the empirical core of the book, and here we present and unpack the findings from interviews, focus groups and document analysis. In Chapter Three, we explore the nature of the governance reforms in more detail, particularly VCS actors' experiences of various multi-agency networks and partnerships. In the first part of the chapter we focus on the horizontal networks at the community level, between VCS organisations and local communities. We investigate the argument that localised and often informal networking generates knowledge and relationships that are crucial in addressing the complex needs of a post-conflict society. The second half of the chapter offers 'a view from the top', reviewing the experiences of 'invited spaces' for government–VCS interaction and formal and informal government–VCS interactions and consultations. While these vertical networks demonstrate government's recognition of the VCS as a legitimate voice in a wide range of policy fields, as we move through the data we will see that questions are raised around the effectiveness of such spaces and the extent to which they are 'box-ticking' affairs with marginal effect on government decision making. We also question the extent to which these spaces for government–VCS engagement and interaction offer a reprieve from the dominance of technocratic and non-confrontational consensus-building practices.

In Chapter Four we explore these concerns in more detail by reviewing the alternative narratives describing the VCS–government relationship. We will see that it seems to be the case that the celebrated networks and partnerships have also induced pragmatic collaboration that is driven simply by funding, and that inter-organisational competition has increased. We will see that a professionalised and financially dependent VCS now often eschews its purportedly grassroots origins in favour of technocratic service delivery. If the VCS has any alternative viewpoints to offer, it appears to be the case that the rigid objectives and fixed priorities of government policymaking rarely bend to incorporate them.

Chapter Five investigates the debates and discussions surrounding independence of voice, purpose and action, and the extent to which the independence of the VCS has been eroding as a result of a 'neoliberal turn' in government–VCS relationships. We will see that organisations are cognizant of the challenges that the new environment poses. In a context in which funding streams are increasingly narrow in their scope, interviewees' reflections suggest that staying true to one's organisational mission and values, and one's freedom to act in innovative, cooperative and locally relevant ways, has become increasingly difficult. We explore wider debates concerning VCS organisations' capacity for 'independent voice' within a contract-driven funding environment, and how these debates have been crystallised by the more recent funding cutbacks and other significant changes in the funding environment. We also explore the ability of the sector to engage politically and offer meaningful alternatives when it is increasingly being positioned as an agent that must work to government's 'predetermined script' (Acheson, 2013, 10).

Given NI's decades-long 'double transition' to peace and neoliberalism (McCabe, 2013, 4) and the sector's extraordinary role in peace programmes, service delivery and state–civil society partnerships (Acheson, 2009, 70), NI provides a particularly interesting context for exploring the role and significance of VCS organisations. As Eikenberry (2009) suggests, there is a history and tradition of critical and normative theorising in the field of voluntary sector studies, and it is within this tradition of critical analysis that we will explore the role of VCS organisations in the particular circumstances of post-peace accord NI. These are turbulent times for the voluntary sector across the UK, and this means we need to be particularly cognisant of the fact that many of the 'emerging' controversies and debates surrounding the VCS are far from new. Therefore, we need to maintain a sense of proportion as we explore the role of the sector and its attempts to navigate this changing environment (Rees and Mullins, 2016, 261; Breeze and Mohan, 2020).

Common-sense understandings of what constitutes 'civil society' or the 'VCS', and the role it can or should play in society, reflect the ideologies, policy goals and discourses of a given time and place. Therefore, the debates surrounding these concepts can be prone to some definitional fuzziness and slippage. The notion of 'civil society' captures a wide range of associational and individual actions in society (Milbourne and Cushman, 2013), including social movements, trade unions and faith communities (Goldstraw, 2018, 616). It also refers to ambiguous concepts such as the 'non-profit sector', 'third sector', 'non-governmental organisations' (NGOs) and the 'VCS', which are often used interchangeably with 'civil society' in policy narratives and scholarship (Wagner, 2012). Perhaps because of its propensity towards such definitional fuzziness, the 'virtues' of civil society have been celebrated since 'the dawn of classical political philosophy' (Davies and Pill, 202, 194) and it is an idea that has been theorised and debated by thinkers from across the political spectrum for centuries (Seligman, 1992; Foley and Edwards, 1998; Kaviraj and Khilnani, 2001; Wagner, 2012). Civil society is a concept that has been embraced by academics, politicians, governments, global institutions, NGOs, philanthropists and the media to legitimate a wide range of political positions. However, in many ways it is wrapped up with ideas concerning political inclusiveness (Harris, 2005, 36),[1] moral obligations and civic virtue (Powell, 2007, 48), as well as sociability, reciprocity and cooperativeness. Just as the idea of a 'flourishing' civil society brings to mind notions of social cohesion and democratic participation, the concept is often used as an ethical ideal or model against which different aspects of existing societies, institutions and practices can be measured (Dekker and van den Broke, 1998, 12; Harris, 2005, 36). As a result, it is unsurprising that one often finds a renewed interest in the idea when there is a perceived 'crisis in the social order' (Seligman, 1992, 15–16).

As Chapters Three, Four and Five will discuss in detail, a moralising deployment of the idea of civil society as a space of voluntary and cooperative citizen participation is particularly relevant to NI. Particularly during and after the peace process, the VCS often seemed to be conflated with civil society (Ketola and Hughes, 2018, 202). Civil society had become something of a synonym for the 'good society' (Coakley and O'Dowd, 2007, 21), and the VCS was seen by itself and others as a key actor in building a new, peaceful NI. Elite-driven political narratives framed NI's civil society as 'a repository of tolerance, non-discrimination, non-violence, trust and cooperation, freedom and democracy', representing it as a sphere of social activity that was characterised by positive norms and values, responsible citizenship (Coakley and O'Dowd, 2007, 21) and political moderation. Indeed, given the significant role afforded to the VCS in governance, advocacy and cross-community relations, there was a general reluctance to criticise the region's VCS organisations (McAreavey, 2017, 166). The discursive positioning of the VCS by sectoral and political elites, their attempts to define the sector's place and role in society, has drawn on both the radical traditions of VCS activity and neoliberal notions of civil society. While the former frames civil society as the foundation for building new alternatives (Edwards, 2009, viii), the latter is concerned with recasting civil society and the VCS as 'just another way of delivering public services' (Acheson, 2014, 293). As will become clear, for many individuals who have reason to think meaningfully about the role and nature of today's VCS, it is this tension between the idea of a radical and provocative sector and a professionalised sector that has been co-opted into state-determined agendas that is at the core of their reflections and concerns.

The shape and size of the VCS in NI

Estimating the true size and shape of the Northern Irish VCS continues to be a challenging task, for any detailed analysis is limited by the nature of the available data. The Charity Commission for Northern Ireland (CCNI) was established in 2009, and until its process for registering charities is completed, it remains difficult to give an accurate picture of the size and shape of the VCS at a given time. For example, the CCNI estimates that there are anywhere between 7,000 and 12,000 charities operating in NI,[2] and there might be 'as many as 10,500 charitable organisations still to be registered'.[3]

The most recent *State of the Sector* report produced by the Northern Ireland Council for Voluntary Action (NICVA) estimated that there are 6,122 organisations in what it terms the 'voluntary, community and social enterprise' sector in NI. Despite some limitations, the *State of the Sector* reports offer some useful insights into ongoing and broader trends within the VCS, and they capture some aspects of the ever-changing nature of the relationship that the sector has with government. Perhaps the most salient trend concerns the steady growth of income received from government sources over the last number of decades, and how this has increased as a proportion of total sectoral income (see also Acheson, 2014). An analysis of the composition of the organisations registered by the CCNI also offers some degree of insight into the shape of the VCS. Notwithstanding the caveats already mentioned about the incompleteness of the current data, it is clear that most organisations have a relatively small annual income, and as is reflected in NICVA's data, a significant share of government funding is directed at a relatively small number of larger organisations involved in the delivery of government contracts and services. Research also suggests that the sector is a significant employer in the region, with NICVA estimating that there are over 53,000 sectoral employees working in a variety of occupational roles.

Data collection

Researching the VCS can be a complex and difficult process. In part this stems from the fact that, despite many efforts to concretise its meaning, the VCS continues to evade precise definitions (Alcock, 2010). This definitional fuzziness, the lack of clarity over its true size and shape, and the fact that much of what we might understand as the 'VCS' lies 'below the radar' of official bodies and researchers (McCabe, Phillimore and Mayblin, 2010), means it is difficult to both fully explore the VCS or make generalisations concerning it.

We draw primarily on data from policy documents, sourced from various government departments both at UK and NI levels, and on data collected through interviews and focus groups held with actors from within the VCS, funding bodies and government. The logic behind choosing these data sources is closely linked with the overarching aims of the book: to present as well as to problematise the varying, and often competing, narratives and understandings of the policy trajectories that the VCS has witnessed over the past number of decades. Key informants were selected because, as a result of their role or social position, they had reason to think meaningfully and critically about the research topics (Gilchrist, 1992; Marshall, 1996). The interview questions required respondents to critically reflect on their own practices, views and experiences, and, therefore, the data captures individual perspectives rather than official, organisational or departmental policy. Our document analysis was partly motivated by a need to understand the governmental logic that drove the wide-reaching reforms to the VCS's relationship with government. In other words, what form did the 'partnership' narrative articulated by UK and NI governments take at different times, and what role did these narratives and their accompanying policies confer on the VCS? Additionally, we were also interested in the VCS's responses to these policy trajectories. How did sectoral representatives interpret the meaning of the policies, how did they respond to them, and what were the real-life effects of these policies for VCS organisations? As a consequence, our interviewees were being asked to reflect on the VCS and the complicated environment it is operating in, and they were asked to reflect on different VCS traditions and complex ideological, normative and political issues. It is only through their nuanced understandings and deep insights into the role and nature of the sector, its relationship with governing institutions and communities, and wider social, economic and political issues in the region, that our study was made possible.

Rolling out neoliberal reforms

At its core, neoliberalism can be understood as a conviction that unregulated open markets, or markets regulated through competition, provide the best possible means for social and economic development. Rhetorically at least, it is predicated on minimal state intervention in the market, and it privileges individual enterprise while steering away from any collective forms of solidarity. The role of the state is seen in terms of negative rights, or a 'freedom from' the state, and the neoliberal state must use its monopoly of the means of violence to protect property rights, free markets and free trade (Harvey, 2007a, 64). For Harvey (2007b, 23), practices at the state level are further anchored in a global set of rules enacted by governments and enforced by intergovernmental agencies, where membership is conditional on accepting these rules. Peck and Tickell (2007), with specific reference to the UK, explore neoliberalism in terms of two phases: the *roll back* of the welfare state through spending cuts and the *roll out* of network governance, re-regulation and the responsibilisation of communities and individuals. These processes open up spaces for the VCS to embrace partnership-working as a non-state delivery agent in a marketised system, while at the same time it is discursively positioned as a champion of individual liberties, self-help, advocacy and social rights.

Such metanarratives are useful shorthand descriptors of broad structural phenomena, but they can be poorly suited to articulating the actually existing practices of neoliberalism on the ground. We therefore begin from the position outlined by Brenner, Peck and Theodore (2010, 332), that neoliberalism always exists in a variegated form. This idea captures how processes of neoliberalisation interact with local political dynamics, inherited social structures and institutions and the local welfare mix, and how neoliberalism cannot exist in a 'purebred' form (Peck, 2013, 145). As Brenner, Peck and Theodore,

(2010, 332) argue, 'neoliberalization tendencies can only be articulated in incomplete, hybrid modalities, which may crystallise in certain regulatory formations, but which are nevertheless continually and eclectically reworked in context-specific ways'. In other words, as Boland (2014, 771) suggests, 'place and politics matter' in processes of neoliberalisation. In another illustration of the hybrid and contingent nature of neoliberalism, Peck (2010) describes it as 'parasitical', in that it is constantly borrowing and extracting from other approaches and ideologies. The importance of context and the scope for localised policy innovations within an overarching neoliberal framework, and the notions of hybridity and 'borrowing', are central to explaining how neoliberal governance plays out in practice. Therefore, they are important anchors for any analysis of the Northern Irish experience.

Neoliberal discourses have increasingly shaped 'the common-sense way we interpret, live in and understand the world' (Harvey, 2006, 145), but again, these discourses are interacting with localised worldviews, understandings, policy narratives and inherited practices. Therefore, we focus on how neoliberal policies and discourses become embedded in a unique local context, but also how their meanings are negotiated in a political environment where a broader neoliberal agenda and powerful neoliberal discourses are constantly meshing with localised exigencies and understandings. As we shall see, rather than viewing neoliberalism as a coherent monolithic system, it is best conceived of as a 'hegemonic restructuring ethos, as a dominant pattern of (incomplete and contradictory) regulatory transformation' (Peck, Theodore and Brenner, 2010). Following Peck (2004, 395), it will become clear in future chapters that despite the 'family resemblances' between neoliberal approaches and discourses, 'local institutional context clearly (and really) matters in the style, substance, origins and outcomes' of neoliberal reform.

These observations suggest that neoliberalism as a concept and ideology needs to be juxtaposed against actually existing neoliberal logics of regulation and governance (Peck, 2013). The early expressions of unapologetic neoliberalism captured in the rhetoric of Margaret Thatcher or in Friedrich Hayek's utopian ideal of a free-market society have given way to contemporary processes of neoliberalism that are rather different in form. The 'rolling back of the state' has in practice entailed a move towards the use of non-state actors in the delivery of core welfare and public-service functions (Herman and Yarwood, 2015), albeit under various forms of government oversight and 'control freakery' (see Davies, 2011a; Davies, 2011b). As a result, despite the considerable effort to transfer responsibility to non-state actors, the extent to which any of this has actually reduced the size of the state remains questionable (Peck, 2004; Peck, 2013). The evidence would rather suggest that the 'rolled-back state' in fact requires sophisticated technologies of governance in order to operationalise the roll back (see Penny, 2017; Davies, 2010). Therefore, rather than getting stuck on questions around the size of the state in a given moment, there may be more interesting questions to ask regarding the interests and ideologies that are served by the neoliberal state and the networks it develops (Davies, 2011a). Peck (2010) has also pointed to new policy innovations that have been designed to manage the costs and contradictions of earlier waves of neoliberalisation. These include shifts from 'dogmatic deregulation to market-friendly reregulation, from structural adjustment to good governance, from budget cuts to regulation-by-audit, from welfare retrenchment to active social policy, from privatisation to public-private partnership, from greed-is-good to markets-with-morals' (Peck, 2010, 106).

The roll out of neoliberal reforms in NI should be understood in this context of continual shifts, innovations and adaptations, and the constant layering of governing complexity in an effort to manage costs and contradictions. As we shall see in the following chapters, drawing on a language of inter-dependencies, coordination, feedback loops, consensus building and dispersed responsibility, neoliberalism fetishises overly complex technocratic solutions to identifiable problems. Concerned with 'government at a distance' (Welsh, 2014, 16) the neoliberal project creates an unnavigable buffer zone between the citizen and the state that is made up of elite-recognised stakeholders and experts. Within this zone of consensual policymaking, politics gives way to policy and 'disruption or dissent is reduced to debates over the institutional modalities of governing, the accountancy calculus of risk, and the technologies of expert administration or management' (Swyngedouw, 2009, 609). It is certainly the case that historical processes and efforts to manage NI's conflicts and divisions have given its governance structures a complicated character. However, with the region's unreserved enthusiasm for neoliberal notions of partnership, cooperativeness and civil society, it has become something of a caricature of the neoliberal tendency towards complexity, technocracy and expert administration. As we reflect on the data outlined in the forthcoming chapters, we also need to bear in mind that, throughout the 2000s, neoliberal governments were committed to building open and decentralised policy-design and implementation systems to address myriad issues around poverty, unemployment and social exclusion. These 'systems' would be responsive to 'learning' garnered from international 'best practice', but above all, government would be unwavering in its refusal 'to accept the conclusion that sustainable responses to underemployment and poverty lie outside the neoliberal policy repertoire' (Peck and Theodore, 2001, 432).

In other words, during the time that the government–VCS relationship was being moulded into its current form, successive Westminster and Northern Irish administrations had relatively immutable boundaries around what policy responses were deemed acceptable or feasible in areas that the VCS was centrally involved in, such as poverty alleviation or unemployment. In such a policymaking environment, even if otherwise inclined, a VCS actor would have to restrict itself to picking at the margins of policy implementation in order to maintain its credibility within the policy community. As our findings will demonstrate, strategically, a disposition that values engagement with governmental 'partners' may have made sense if one believed government's promises of partnership, consultation and participation in 'shared decision making', and it may have made sense when there existed a steady stream of funding from a range of sources for VCS activities. However, as we shall discuss in forthcoming chapters, this disposition towards partnership and consensus may be a hindrance when the policy and financial environment begins to change.

We also need to bear in mind from the outset that NI, particularly after the peace process, was being bombarded by powerful discourses around the importance of partnership, participation and social capital. In the social capital and wider 'connectionist' literature (see Davies, 2011a), networks arise out of the fact that government and other elites will recognise that a variety of interests and agencies are all trying to deal with similar problems and that these efforts need some level of coordination. With coordination through negotiation, debate and the building of trust and consensus, 'partnership' can, according to the theory, 'eliminate nugatory effort' (Davies, 2010, 84). Invariably, in environments that value collaboration, different agencies must have repeated interactions as they meet to 'exchange resources and negotiate shared purposes' (Rhodes, 1997, 53). In connectionist discourses, these networked relationships will be sustained by affective trust (norms and values) and instrumental trust (i.e. opportunities for free-riding or competitive advantage will be rejected in the hope of future collaborative effort) (Davies, 2011a, 66). Interactions in networks also come to be rooted in trust as network participants build on past successes and come to recognise that they are dependent on each other to achieve shared goals. Previous collaborative successes, in other words, create a 'cultural template for future collaboration'

(Putnam, 1995, 67). Government's role, according to this narrative, is to define the problems, facilitate the linkages that can help deal with the problem, encourage innovation and coordinate the development of a shared vision and shared sense of purpose among the diverse partners (Pierre and Stoker, 2002, 29–39). With each collaborative success, a diverse range of actors can become locked into a cycle of virtuous returns as they build on past achievements. This would suggest that even if relationships are instrumentally or funding driven, the norms of cooperation, the community-level relationships and social capital will be constantly reinforced. However, as will become clear, many sectoral interviewees' experiences would seem to invalidate this positive reading of partnership, networking and funding-driven cooperation.

The VCS has also served as a site for promoting self-help or market-based 'solutions' to complex problems, and as a site for garnering widespread 'buy-in' to norms and values that align with the worldview, dispositions and behaviours deemed appropriate under neoliberal citizenship (see Wilkins, 2018). As a result, instead of 'a clear distinction between the values and practices of (quasi) state and voluntary welfare organisations' there has often been a 'convergence in the discursive framing [of need and welfare] and governmental technologies of state, for-profit, and voluntary welfare providers' (May et al, 2019, 1254). For researchers, this brings up the question of whether the apparent institutional buy-in to neoliberal and communitarian discourses in the VCS is part of a cynical process of pragmatically playing the 'funding game', or whether there has been a very real process of cultural and attitudinal change that goes beyond the merely discursive. In other words, does the sector hold on to some of the 'unruly, grassroots, ethical and subversive' (DeVerteuil, 2017, 1520) worldviews and dispositions that it sees itself as possessing. These are questions that we return to over the next few chapters.

Governance in times of peace and conflict

It is also important at the outset to be conscious of the extraordinary role that the sector has played in the governance of NI (McCall and Williamson, 2001), as well as the extraordinary discourses that have surrounded it. The role of the VCS in the peace process, particularly in facilitating the distribution of external resources, is intricately linked to broader technologies of neoliberal governance that came to inform the transition to peace before and after the GFA. This built on the privileged role the VCS played during the Troubles, when, following the suspension of the devolved administration, a close relationship between civil servants and the VCS grew around a shared interest in maintaining the core functions of public administration (Acheson and Milofsky, 2008; Acheson, 2009). Despite the fact that the VCS was and continues to be divided along the main ethno-religious lines of Protestant/unionist and Catholic/nationalist, its role as a valued partner in peacebuilding was rarely in doubt (DHSS, 1993; DSD, 2003). By the 1990s, civil-society organisations saw themselves, and were seen by government, as one of the vehicles for achieving a more peaceful and stable NI (Acheson, Milofsky and Stringer, 2011). Indeed, the pre-GFA era might be best described as a series of 'covert and not so covert attempts to recruit elements of civil society' to the management of conflict (Acheson, 2010, 177).

Following the signing of the GFA in 1998, there was a clear rhetorical commitment on the part of government to the VCS. At this time, NI was enjoying a flood of international and UK funding for peace programmes that supported the rapid growth (McCall and Williamson, 2001, 364) and professionalisation of the sector, and this was bolstered by the New Labour reforms that were championing the value of civil society. Simultaneously, the peace agreement was to be primarily bolstered by a 'liberalisation jamboree' (Horgan, 2006, 665) of economic aid, but also the promotion of free markets and the concomitant liberal democratic norms and values. It was certainly the case that the VCS and broader civil society were seen as key players in instilling these new norms and values in wider society, and they were positioned as 'leaders by example'. These kinds of overblown references to the VCS's role in peacebuilding have been excised from the governing 'script' in more recent years (Acheson, 2013, 10), therefore, in the following chapters we explore what kinds of new stories and organising discourses surround the VCS.

TWO

Neoliberal enrolment? The 'partnership turn' in government rhetoric and policy

In recent decades, the political mainstreams of western democracies and transnational institutions have increasingly seen civil-society institutions (Davies and Pill, 2012, 193), civil society–state partnerships (Davies, 2011a, 41) and the development of a renewed sense of community as part of 'the answer to the challenges of a changing world' (Blair, 2000, cited in Levitas, 2000, 189). In policy terms this signalled a 'turn' to partnership and 'network governance' (Davies, 2011a, 41), and successive administrations in the UK, together with their quasi-independent think tanks (Levitas, 2005, 168), identified the VCS as a potential site for cheaper, alternative and innovative ways of delivering public services and regenerating communities (see Milbourne, 2013, 37). Through a process of 'moral hectoring and mild coercion' (Kearns, 1995, 158), these administrations promoted the idea of a self-governing and depoliticised 'active citizen' that is aware of their responsibilities and obligations to themselves, their neighbours, their community and the nation (Davies, 2011a). Civil society, and the VCS in particular, was hailed as the answer to the 'wicked problems' of increasing social fragmentation, growing polarisation between the rich and the poor (Milbourne, 2013) and the (alleged) breakdown of a sense of community and moral responsibility in communities that were perceived to be deficient, deviant and dependent (Imrie and Raco, 2003, 7; Leonard, 2004, 928).

Over the decades, governments across the political spectrum 'elevated certain charitable entities as partners in the business of public welfare' (Corcoran, 2017, 287), and the organised sector came to be seen as a key player in governance and service delivery because, it was claimed, it had the potential to deliver new and innovative solutions to social challenges (see Brown, 2006, in Haugh and Kitson, 2007, 986). Reflecting a convergence of different political and sectoral interests, by the late 1990s policy narratives were promoting the notion of a single, distinct and coherent 'third sector' that could be an object and instrument of policy (Kendall, 2000; Imrie and Raco, 2003; Carmel and Harlock, 2008; Acheson, 2010), and this discursive framing helped to secure the VCS's political and financial support and temporarily mask some of its internal tensions and divisions (Alcock, 2010, 19). Over the coming decades, policymakers, academics and think tanks would explore mechanisms for developing a more supportive environment for VCS activity, ways of improving coordination and collaboration between government and the VCS, and policy incentives that would 'nudge' individuals and communities in the direction of voluntary and community action (Smith and Jones, 2015, 235).

The Conservative Party and the 'partnership turn'

Much of the political focus on the VCS reflects the fact that, from Thatcher and John Major to Tony Blair and Gordon Brown, and on to David Cameron and Theresa May, British governments have believed that volunteering, 'community', and civil-society institutions could all play a role in wider processes of neoliberal 'modernisation' and reform. As Clarke et al (2000, 20) explain in relation to New Labour's modernisation agenda, social-service reforms can be accompanied by a legitimising 'discourse of failure, directed at both previous governments and the social services themselves'. This is often coupled with nostalgic lamentations over a supposedly lost 'special something' in the character, morals and values of society, the rediscovery and restoration of which has the potential to inspire national revival (see Crawford, 2001). The discourses of state failure, and nostalgia about the past, are not isolated to New Labour. Neoliberal advocates across the globe have pointed to governments' failure to provide for marginalised and vulnerable groups and communities as evidence that the institutions of a 'monolithic' state are too expensive, inefficient, inconsistent, intrusive, inflexible and bureaucratic to effectively and efficiently meet society's needs. Depending on the rhetorical fashions of the time, it has been argued by such proponents of neoliberalism that the empowerment of individuals and communities, communal and individual self-help, self-reliance and resilience, Victorian-like philanthropic whims and beneficence, social enterprise and entrepreneurialism, and the 'social capital' of the VCS, can be the driving forces behind more effective and efficient ways to address social issues and needs.

In the UK, the Conservative Party's rhetoric in the early years of Thatcher's leadership suggested support for the 'Victorian values' of 'selflessness and benefaction' (Thatcher, 1977) and support for the volunteer associations that were a 'vital part' of the 'defence of our freedom of action' (Thatcher, 1981, cited in Acheson and Williamson, 1995, 38). The Conservative governments of the 1980s were also committed to a 'moralisation of the individual' (Imrie and Raco, 2003, 11), promoting the idea that it is our duty to look after ourselves and our neighbours (Thatcher, 1987) by becoming active and responsible citizens (Hurd, 1989, cited in Kearney, 1995, 42; Davies, 2011a, 42), and they encouraged private charitable giving (Robson, 1989; Smith, 2007). With Thatcher's critique of the public sector and eagerness 'to limit the growth of public welfare provision' (Harris, 2010, 36), the voluntary and private sectors were seen as potential sources of alternative and lower-cost services (Plowden, 2003; 415; Cunningham and Nickson, 2011, 663). It was during this time that the VCS and the state began entering into (sometimes uneasy) partnerships in a range of policy areas (Crowson, 2011, 496).

The Thatcherite project was concerned with the rolling back of the state, the hollowing out of state services (Acheson, 1995, 34) and the promotion of informal, localised and private voluntarism rather than a more institutionalised form of voluntary action (see Corbett and Walker, 2012; Lindsey et al, 2018). With the sector 'seen more as a market alternative to state welfare' than as a genuine partner (Alcock, 2010, 20), and with a fear among the Conservative leadership that support for voluntarism might produce 'an alternative social and political power base' for protest movements (Lindsey et al, 2018, 24), the political rhetoric about voluntarism and community rarely translated into supportive policy programmes, institutional support or positive engagement with the VCS (see Imrie and Raco, 2003; Lindsey et al, 2018). The increasing involvement of voluntary-sector providers in contractual service delivery and quasi-markets in the 1980s and 1990s raised fears about the instrumentalisation or agentification of the sector and the development of a 'contract culture' and a government agenda that appeared to ignore the sector's purportedly distinctive 'values' (see Lewis, 1999; Plowden, 2003; Macmillan, 2010; Crowson, 2011). Voluntary organisations were increasingly taking over responsibility for delivering mainstream services instead of complementing and supplementing the services provided by the statutory sector (Harris et al, 2001, 3), and advocates of neoliberalism were suggesting that voluntary action and 'community' were acceptable substitutes for state activities (Deakin, 2001, 27; see also Hoggett, 1997, 10; Lindsey et al, 2018, 21).

After Thatcher's resignation, Conservative administrations continued to pursue neoliberal policies, 'albeit without the hectoring tone' and charisma of their former leader (Jessop, 2015, 21). However, by the mid-1990s, worries about the socially erosive effects of unconstrained markets (Cochrane, 1999), a desire to build a new social 'consensus' after the political turmoil of the 1980s (Davies, 2011a, 42) and questions regarding standards and accountability in a marketised service-delivery system, prompted gradual changes of direction in government policy and language (Deakin, 2001; Davies, 2011a). In the area of service delivery, there was a recognition of the distinctive organisational cultures in the VCS and the need for minimum standards (Deakin, 2001, 27), and reviews of statutory–voluntary sector relationships urged government to recognise the VCS's advocacy role and to take an interest in its overall 'well-being' (Lewis, 1999, 263; Dunn, 2000, 148; Dunn, 2006). In the area of regeneration and community development, there was a discursive shift towards partnership, community participation and empowerment (Osbourne and Ross, 2001, 83; Imrie and Raco, 2003, 3; Davies, 2011a, 41), and the Major government's strategies supported voluntarism as a driver of social engagement and active citizenship (Selman and Parker, 1997, 173; Lindsey et al, 2018, 25). Additionally, there was increasingly a belief that there was a need to develop more effective mechanisms for coordination between diverse actors with the emergence of a 'polycentric state' (Rhodes, 1996, 657).

The state-backed regeneration efforts of the early and mid-1990s stressed 'the need for tripartite partnerships between the public, private and community sectors' (Foley and Martin, 2000, 481) and these collaborations marked a discursive shift away from confrontation to consensus building, a shift that was perhaps made easier by the defeat of the unions and Left-wing local governments in the mid-1980s (Davies, 2011a, 47; Milbourne, 2013). These funding programmes sought to instil 'connectionist' (Davies, 2011a, 5) norms and practices, for at the local level different agencies would have to come together as 'partnerships' (Morrison, 2005, 145). Simultaneously, the programmes also sought to instil competitive norms and practices, for the partnerships would have to bid to receive funding in competition with other localities (see Atkinson, 1999, 63; Foley and Martin, 2000, 481; Imrie and Raco, 2003, 12; Morrison, 2005, 145). By the time New Labour came to power in 1997, there were questions around the success of such area-based initiatives 'in addressing neighbourhood disadvantage' (Pill, 2012, 77), and though the notions of citizen involvement and 'partnership' had become political mantras (Fordham et al, 1999), the VCS and communities lacked the power and influence enjoyed by businesses and public agencies (Morrison, 2005, 145). As a result, they played little or no role in agenda setting or decision making, and communities were 'only consulted at a relatively late stage about a narrow range of options which had already been formulated by other "partners"' (Foley and Martin, 2000, 481). In addition, in the area of service delivery, there were continued debates and concerns about sectoral independence and a 'contract culture' (Rees and Mullins, 2016). It was in this context that the incoming New Labour government would commit itself to avoiding the mistakes of the 'collaborative' projects it would inherit from the Conservative administration (Imrie and Raco, 2003, 12), and having vowed to 'replace a contract culture with a partnership culture' while in opposition, it promised that it would genuinely empower communities and ensure the independence of the VCS (see Plowden, 2003, 419).

New Labour and the third way

New Labour policies are particularly important in the context of NI, because although The GFA was signed in 1998, creating the power-sharing Northern Ireland Executive and the elected Northern Ireland Assembly (otherwise known as Stormont), these institutions were suspended between 2002 and 2007 (Acheson and Milofsky, 2008, 75). Therefore, the VCS in NI and its relationship with government were in many ways moulded into their current form under the New Labour direct-rule interregnum (see Acheson, 2013, 10). As New Labour had such a profound influence on the role and nature of today's VCS and its relationship with the state, and as the sector was a prominent player in community-relations strategies that were introduced by the British government in the absence of a local assembly (Campbell et al, 2008, 23), we need to explore in some detail the ideological drivers behind New Labour's third-way agenda and the relationship this engendered between the VCS and the state.

Since New Labour's landslide victory in 1997, there has been much debate as to whether its third-way policy agenda and its associated discourses represented 'an elaborate rhetorical device' that sought to 'legitimise the capitulation of the Centre-Left to the triumph of neo-liberal ideology', or if it represented a shift in Centre-Left strategy that reflected new social, economic and political realities (see Leggett, 2004, 187). As Powell's (2000, 44) concise exploration of some of the key themes in the early years of its administration suggests, New Labour sought 'to move from a passive to an active, preventive welfare state', and there was a focus on human capital investment, education, a better distribution of opportunities, government partnerships with business and civil society, 'wise' rather than 'big' public spending, labour-market inclusion as a mechanism for social inclusion and a 'rights with responsibilities' policy discourse (see also Davies, 2011a, 42). There was also a neoliberal-communitarian tendency to frame the relationship between citizen and state in contractual terms (see Schinkel and van Houdt, 2010, 699), with the deployment of political discourses that sought to make rights, and access to resources and support, contingent on individuals and communities living up to their side of a state-determined bargain (see Powell, 2000, 47; Raco and Flint, 2001, 596; Hastings, 2003, 99; Corcoran, 2017, 290). Of course, this New Labour agenda was influenced by 'contradictory and conflicting' traditions (Lister, 2003, 438), and an awareness of these different influences helps us to not lose sight of the nuances within and between different periods and fields of policymaking (see Hesmondhalgh et al, 2015). Additionally, at times New Labour's overall political and economic project reflected the tensions between the main protagonists in the leadership, and any coherence in the programme was betrayed by periods of 'policymaking on the hoof' (Powell, 2000, 53), 'policy-churning' and ongoing responses to a succession of failed initiatives (Jessop, 2007, 287).

However, whatever the influences on New Labour rhetoric and policymaking, it soon became clear that their electoral victory did not signal a reversal of the changes made to the British economy and society by the previous Conservative governments (Jessop, 2003, 1). The New Labour leadership did not set out to reverse the Thatcherite settlement (see Davies, 2011a, 45–7), and it reproduced the Conservative government's mantra that 'overall economic growth would filter down to enhance opportunities for those at the bottom of society' (Milbourne, 2013, 37). Business was 'over-represented in scores of official review and advisory bodies' amid increasing privatisation of public and social services (Jessop, 2003, 10), and in line with its neoliberal leanings, the party's policy narratives had a tendency to give longstanding ideas a market inflection (see Hall, 2011, 711). Much of this third-way agenda was the culmination of extensive ideological shifts and changes in electoral strategy under successive Labour leaderships (see Hay, 1999; Levitas, 2005; Davies, 2011a). As the common goal of electoral success often outweighed any ideological divisions (Levitas, 2005, 1), many of those on the already demoralised political Left (Davies 2004, 576; Davies, 2011a, 47) kept their opposition to the New Labour leadership's agenda muted.

Fundamentally, third-way politics would not mark a decisive break with the neoliberal reforms of the 1980s and 1990s (Davies, 2005, 316; Newman, 2005, 719), for New Labour took the economic and political legacies of Thatcherism as 'irreversible faits accomplis' (Jessop, 2015, 22), and its overall aim was the transformation of 'nation and people to fit them for a globalised world that required workforce flexibility, business deregulation' and the 'modernisation' of the welfare state (Newman, 2005, 719). The state would still be represented as too universal, expensive, intrusive, inflexible and bureaucratic (see Fairclough, 2000; Powell, 2000; Deakin, 2001; Newman, 2001; Imrie and Raco, 2003; Hodgson, 2004), and the party would continue to disassociate itself from 'old Labour' forms of statism (Hodgson, 2004, 141; Milbourne, 2013, 37). However, reflecting the influence of different communitarian thinkers on the New Labour project (Levitas, 2000; Alcock and Scott, 2002, 114), and 'Blair's strong Christian socialist leanings' (Jessop, 2003, 4), New Labour also claimed that they did not support the free-market dogmas and competitive individualism of the past, because such an agenda would continue to have an erosive effect on the notions of social responsibility, citizenship and civic engagement (Imrie and Raco, 2003, 7; Levitas, 2005, 113). Hence, a focus on the idea of 'community', rather than 'society', was to become central to communicating the third-way agenda's 'difference both from the neo-liberal New Right and from forms of socialism dependent on intervention by the state' (Levitas, 2000, 191).

With the sector being 'explicitly neither state nor market' (Lindsey et al, 2018, 26), it was to become central to the narratives New Labour would construct to distance themselves from the 'crude individualism' (Heron and Dwyer, 1999, 93) and state withdrawal of the 1980s, as well as Labour's historical association with centralised public services. In line with intellectual fashions of the time, certain variants of mainstream social capital theory (see Putnam, 2000; Field, 2003; Halpern, 2005; Fine, 2010) were a perfect framework for New Labour, for these theories exhibited a discomfort with adversarial politics, celebrated sociability and voluntarism and had a distaste for traditional solidarities (Hughes, 2015, 25). These theories, with their functionalist (Siisiäinen, 2000, 16) and neoliberal origins (Fine, 2010, 48), were preoccupied with the question of how to cultivate trust-based networks, societal consensus and social integration, but they did so without questioning the underlying structures of the society that communities and individuals are being integrated into (see Siisiäinen, 2000; Fine, 2010; Davies, 2011a). As Kearns (2003, 38) argues, this focus on social capital and social exclusion allowed New Labour to perform a discursive shift away from poverty and the functioning of the economy onto 'soft' issues like family, participation and self-esteem.

Committed to a pluralist and market-driven approach to welfare delivery (Milbourne, 2013), and to a programme that would reduce 'the public sector's share in the direct or indirect provision of goods and services' (Jessop, 2003, 5), New Labour offered the sector a central role in governance, service delivery and area-based regeneration (Lewis, 2005; Davies, 2011a; Milbourne, 2013; Buckingham and Rees, 2016). Such a policy programme required some sort of organising narrative, and for New Labour this would revolve around the idea of 'partnership'. Networks and partnerships made up of multiple actors would be a 'new paradigm' for policymaking and service delivery (Newman, 2001, 104), and the celebration and cultivation of such networks became central to 'UK public policy and the New Labour project' (Davies, 2012a, 2688). According to New Labour, the modernisation of public services required more effective collaboration and coordination in service delivery and decision making, the 'joining up' of the resources, talents and competencies of actors from different sectors, and a renewed focus on overcoming organisational or sectoral silos (see Blair, 1999, quoted in Alcock and Kendall, 2010, 6; Foley and Martin, 2000; Alcock and Scott, 2002; Clark, 2002; Lowndes and Sullivan, 2004; Davies, 2005; Pill, 2012; Rees, 2014). In New Labour ideology, only partnership between civil society and government could deal with the social fragmentation, exclusion, anomie, inequality and sense of powerlessness in some of Britain's neighbourhoods (Imrie and Raco, 2003, 7).

With promises that the VCS would have access to more resources and more influence in decision making (Milbourne, 2013), and with a suggestion that the VCS was the 'home' of innovative, responsive, specialist and more-trusted services (see Popple and Redmond, 2000; Haugh and Kitson, 2007; Macmillan, 2010; Teasdale et al, 2012; Macmillan, 2016; Taylor et al, 2016), New Labour's agenda was largely welcomed by many VCS leaders and community activists (Davies, 2011; Alcock, 2016b; Corcoran et al, 2018). New Labour committed itself to avoiding the mistakes of the 'collaborative' projects it had inherited from Conservative administrations (Imrie and Raco, 2003, 12); it initiated 'high-level reviews' on the role of the sector in regeneration and service delivery (Lindsey et al, 2018, 27) and introduced 'a national Compact in England to provide a framework for dealings between central government departments and third sector organisations' (Alcock, 2016a, 32). There was also a renewed emphasis on building a 'professionalised' sector that had the capacity to work in partnership with government, compete for contracts, and efficiently and effectively deliver services (see Carmel and Harlock,

2008; Maguire, 2012, 2; Rees, 2014, 53; Rees and Mullins, 2016, 7; Corcoran et al, 2018, 189; Lindsey et al, 2018, 27).

However, as organisations in the VCS began to become more involved in contracted service delivery within a competitive environment, concerns were raised about sectoral independence and state co-option, the levels of top-down regulation, bureaucracy and prescriptiveness associated with contracts, and the potential for VCS organisations to lose their distinctive cultures and values (Carmel and Harlock, 2008; Chew and Osborne, 2009; Cunningham and James, 2009; Macmillan, 2010; Milbourne, 2013; Milbourne and Cushman, 2013; Alcock, 2016a). There was a concern that New Labour were taking the opportunity to reduce the cost of providing services and passing responsibilities and risks down to the VCS, communities and citizens (Popple and Redmond, 2000; Kisby, 2010; Milbourne and Cushman, 2013), while simultaneously keeping overall control at the 'centre' through contracting, monitoring, target-setting, regulation and an entrenched culture of 'control freakery' (Carmel and Harlock, 2008; Davies, 2008; Davies, 2009a; Buckingham and Rees, 2016). It also appeared to be the case that their rhetorical nods towards social stability, cohesion, civil society and community were being driven by a need to ameliorate the socially erosive and fragmenting effects of neoliberalisation, inequality, individualism and competition (Davies, 2011a; Jessop, 2015), with civil-society activity, volunteering, social capital and charitable giving being framed as 'compensatory measures' and 'quick-fix solutions' for long-term structural problems and inadequate material resources (Leonard, 2004, 928; Lindsey et al, 2018, 28). Despite these concerns, the New Labour years were to be experienced as a period of 'stability and growth' by some voluntary organisations (Hemmings, 2017, 52). However, in the wake of the financial crisis and the election of a Tory-led Conservative–Liberal Democrat Coalition government, issues of funding, sectoral independence, and the role of the VCS and voluntarism in society, were put firmly back on the agenda.

Decoupling from the 'mini public sector': the Coalition and Conservative administrations' approach to the VCS

Following the 2008 financial crisis, neoliberalism would morph into a more extreme and punitive form as 'the costs of restructuring and insecurity were visited (once again) on the poor and the vulnerable' through austerity measures and welfare cuts (Peck, 2013, 136).

Governments across the globe implemented a new round of 'crisis-propelled' austerity, with policy agendas illustrating neoliberal governments' 'high tolerance for job loss and cuts to wages, pensions, and benefits, concomitant with a shrinking public sector and the privatisation of individual risk' (Baines and Cunningham, 2015, 185). In the UK, this more extreme and punitive form of neoliberalism would be managed by the Conservative Party after they came to power as part of a Conservative–Liberal Democrat Coalition in 2010. The party sought to resurrect the Thatcherite agenda, and just as during the Thatcher administration, there would be privatisation of profits, socialisation of losses and a policy agenda that ensured that 'private affluence is secured on the back of public squalor' (Jessop, 2015, 17).

The Conservatives sought to make substantial reductions in public expenditure as part of their deficit-reducing measures (Lindsey et al, 2018, 31), but they also made pre-election promises to empower communities and revitalise a voluntary sector that was 'underused, undervalued and controlled like a "mini public sector"' (see Conservative Party, 2008, 56; Macmillan, 2010, 8). Thus, it was envisioned that state retrenchment would be 'compensated for by a "renewal" of community spirit, voluntary activity and a new breed of social entrepreneurs' (Corbett and Walker, 2012, 488). As suggested in the discussion concerning New Labour, the Conservatives were also keen to distinguish themselves and their agenda from opposition parties, past Tory administrations and their 'nasty party' image. Moreover, like their New Labour predecessors, the Conservatives also needed an organising narrative for their 'new' governing project. This took the form of the 'Big Society', which promised more devolution and 'localism', a shift in power away from central government, the freeing of citizens and organisations from a 'big state' and bureaucracy and the removal of barriers that prevented citizens and communities participating in public services and decision making (see Kisby, 2010; Westwood, 2011; Bach, 2012; Davies and Pill, 2012; Ishkanian and Szreter, 2012; Lowndes and Pratchett, 2012; Teasdale et al, 2012; Buckingham and Rees, 2016; Corcoran, 2017; Dagdeviren et al, 2019).

Just as with New Labour's calls for civil renewal, the Conservatives also wanted to re-engineer society so as to revive the civic pride, sense of social responsibility and communal bonds that had allegedly been lost in deprived communities. Once again, their 'compassionate conservatism' rebranding efforts would include a celebration of civil society (Davies and Pill, 2012, 193). Indeed, the Big Society had significant continuities with New Labour's third way, in that it reflected a mix of thinkers and traditions (Lindsey et al, 2018, 31), and the attempt to roll out the agenda exposed tensions between the different philosophies and traditions at work in the party (Teasdale et al, 2012). There was also a similar 'commitment to decentralisation' (Clayton et al, 2016, 724), and the ideas behind it were consistent with New Labour's view that the market, charities, communities and volunteers might be better than a supposedly over-large and overbearing state (see Kisby, 2010, 484). As with the third way, the voluntary sector and 'community' would continue to be positioned as an important site for civic engagement and participation (Westwood, 2011, 694; Lowndes and Pratchett, 2012, 31; Lowndes and Gardner, 2016), and there would be support for volunteering and community-organising initiatives (Paine and Hill, 2016, 130; Lindsey et al, 2018, 31).[1] Essentially, the Big Society was a legitimating narrative that disguised state retrenchment, marketisation and budget cuts (Bach, 2012; Ishkanian and Szreter, 2012), and as Dagdeviren et al (2019, 144) suggest, it represented another instance of an 'empowerment narrative' being 'deployed to legitimise the severe retrenchment of welfare and other public spending'. As Kisby (2010, 490) predicted, the Big Society faded away, and it would 'soon only be mentioned with an accompanying snigger at its intellectual vacuity'. By 2012, the concept was being quietly abandoned and 'largely expunged from government description of its policies and programmes' (Buckingham and Rees, 2016, 45).

Any initial enthusiasm in the VCS for the Big Society agenda and its civil-society boosterism soon dissipated when the Conservatives sought to financially 'decouple' government from a VCS that had, in the Conservatives' view, developed a 'creeping dependence' on the state (see Macmillan, 2013; Buckingham and Rees, 2016). There was to be a move away from the New Labour 'partnership governance' model and their use of initiatives that were designed to build up the capacity of the VCS (Lindsey et al, 2018, 37). Austerity policies created a complicated picture in terms of the overall distribution of funds to VCS organisations (see Kendall et al, 2018, 761) and there would be more of an emphasis on volunteers, rather than paid staff, becoming involved in the delivery of services (Buckingham and Rees, 2016; Aiken and Harris, 2017; Aiken and Taylor, 2019). The tenor and terms of the new relationship were captured succinctly by Corcoran et al (2019, 97), with the authors observing that after 2010 'the language of partnership, state–voluntary sector "compacts" and parity of esteem gave way to an emphatically marketised, competitive and target-led approach'. Amid severe cuts to welfare budgets, new public-management approaches that stressed competition and 'the importation of techniques from business' (Body and Kendall, 2020, 16) were applied to the VCS in 'insensitive and crude' ways (Pape et al, 2020, 242). The VCS had to manage greater competition with, and at times government preference for, private providers (Teasdale et al, 2012, 208; Rees and Mullins, 2016, 257). To varying extents, VCS organisations also had to manage increasing levels of financial and reputational risk (Taylor et al, 2016, 175), changes in the nature of the relationship between VCS organisations (Ketola and Hughes, 2016; Egdell and Dutton, 2017), hierarchical prime-contractor and supply-chain models (Buckingham and Rees, 2016, 50; Rees and Mullins, 2016, 2; Corcoran et al, 2019, 97), resource-intensive bidding processes and payment by results (Ketola and Hughes, 2016; Taylor et al, 2016, 175).

Accelerating processes put in place by New Labour, a key part of the Conservatives' agenda was a renewed focus on 'choice', improving performance through competition, and diversifying the range of public service providers by enhancing the role of the voluntary, community, social enterprise and private sectors (Teasdale et al, 2012; Clayton et al, 2016). With the Conservative government's privileging of the market as the organising mechanism for the distribution of resources (Baines and Cunningham, 2015; Egdell and Dutton, 2017; Ketola and Hughes, 2018), public services were opened up to competition at unprecedented scales (Lindsey et al, 2018, 34). The policy direction since 2010 has renewed longstanding debates concerning the role of the state *and* the VCS in shifting services and responsibilities away from democratically accountable bodies (Bach, 2012, 404), and renewed concerns about the VCS's potential to become 'a "Trojan horse" for privatisation' (Rees and Mullins, 2016, 2) or a vulnerable 'vacuum filler' in a new period of 'roll-back' neoliberalism (Aiken and Harris, 2017, 338; Dagdeviren et al, 2019, 147; Hughes, 2019). It has also ignited yet another round of debates about the VCS's independence and its relationship with the state (Acheson, 2013; Panel on the Independence of the Voluntary Sector, 2014; Ketola and Hughes, 2016). As Acheson (2014, 294) has illustrated, the research literature at the time captured some of the processes of sectoral resistance against government's broader policy agenda and its specific agenda as regards the VCS, but also a sense of powerlessness and abandonment (see Acheson, 2014, 294; Clayton et al, 2016).

The VCS in NI

As illustrated in previous sections, when researching the VCS, the discourses surrounding the VCS and its role in society, it is important to provide a historical context for empirical data that has been collected over a shorter period, as this allows continuities and changes over time to be made more visible (Milbourne, 2013, 50). The remainder of this chapter will explore the historical role of the VCS in NI and its relationship with the state, and it will sketch out some of the key developments in what is a long history of philanthropy and voluntary action. As we explore these developments, we will see how the VCS came to be shaped by a complex mix of Westminster policy, EU peace and development programmes, social, economic and political processes that were specific to NI, and the policy goals of direct rule and devolved administrations. As will become clear, the VCS's role and nature was influenced, to varying extents, by the neoliberal agendas and policy discourses outlined in previous sections. However, as with so many areas of policymaking in the region, within governance structures there can be a 'clever engagement with neoliberal priorities' (see Hughes et al, 2016, 1095), and processes of 'indigenous policy evolution' (Hodgett and Johnson, 2001, 331) within a general neoliberal framework. Echoing Brenner, Peck and Theodore's (2010) notions of 'variegated neoliberalism', this has tended to give a regionally-specific flavour to the discourses and policy goals that shaped the VCS into its current form.

It is important to note at the outset that, historically, civil society, philanthropy and voluntary action on the island of Ireland have tended to reflect its ethnic, religious and political divisions and its sectarian geographies (Acheson et al, 2005; Acheson, 2009). Before and after partition, structures for voluntary action were generally embedded within the two ethno-religious communities, and just as with other communally-based institutions, both communities strongly identified with 'their' voluntary organisations (Acheson et al, 2006). In the north, there were periodic attempts to develop 'a non-affiliated voluntary sphere' in the earlier decades of the 20th century. However, these efforts struggled to attract members from both communities, and non-denominational organisations were rare because a lack of religious affiliation made it difficult to build support and patronage relationships (Acheson et al, 2005, 192; Heenan and Birrell, 2011, 12). In the first few decades after partition, the voluntary sector played the central role in organising welfare and self-help, and during and after the Second World War its role was influenced by state policies such as the establishment of the National Health Service (see Kearney, 1995; Acheson et al, 2005; Heenan and Birrell, 2011).

In the 1960s and early 1970s, many VCS groups emerged within both Protestant/unionist and Catholic/nationalist working-class areas. These groups were often a defensive response to increasing inter-community conflict (Griffiths, 1975), and they reflected grassroots efforts to address the social needs that arose out of the intensifying level of violence and the resulting population displacement (Kilmurray, 2017, 31). The community groups aimed to provide community-based mutual aid, and while some played a vigilante role within the community, in many cases the groups would replace poorly functioning state services or services that were no longer seen as acceptable or legitimate (see Cochrane, 2000; Birrell and Williamson, 2001; Acheson et al, 2005; Kilmurray, 2017). In some areas of NI, activists from across the political divide worked together as part of inter-community efforts to alleviate sectarian conflict and tensions (Kilmurray, 2017, 43). The spate of conflict-driven grassroots mobilisation, and the move to creating sustainable structures of community development, was more pronounced and rapid in Catholic working-class areas, with the Protestant community experiencing 'greater difficulty in moving out of defensively orientated forms of voluntary action' (Acheson et al, 2005, 198).

However, it was during this period of intense conflict that community development would emerge as a distinctive sphere of VCS activity across the north (Acheson et al, 2005, 198), and developments at that time set in motion the processes that would lead to both the creation of the VCS peace and reconciliation industry, and the significant role that the VCS would play in local governance. In the late 1960s, the unionist government had established the Ministry for Community Relations and a Community Relations Commission, ostensibly for the purposes of developing community-relations policy and delivering community-relations activity (Griffiths, 1972, 128; Birrell and Williamson, 2001, 207). The Community Relations Commission gave help and support to many VCS groups and its funding often supported community development approaches (Fitzduff, 1995, 63), though it was often viewed with suspicion by groups in both communities due to its 'colonizing role' (Birrell and Williamson, 2001, 207). Reflecting government's proactive approach to strengthening civil society in the form of the VCS (Acheson et al, 2004, 189), and reflecting the longstanding belief in governmental and activist circles that 'the people' of NI were 'moderate' in comparison to their more extreme political representatives (Dixon, 1997, 9), since the 1980s the VCS has been the beneficiary of many programmes and funding streams as government and other actors searched for 'bottom-up' ways to promote political stability. The VCS became a major channel for funds from London, the EU and other international funders, and the VCS became a major player in the implementation of programmes and policies (McCall and Williamson, 2001, 364). By this time, the VCS was becoming dependent on funding from governmental and philanthropic organisations (McCall and O'Dowd, 2008, 33), and its activities were nudged in specific directions as VCS groups were 'weaned on a diet of government and EU funding' (Knox and Quirk, 2016, 261–262).

Through the 1980s and 1990s, the role and nature of the VCS to some extent mirrored broader trends in Britain and the moves to a 'mixed economy' in service provision, with the VCS's functions becoming more formalised, more institutionalised and less contentious (Birrell and Williamson, 2001, 209). However, reflective of the extraordinary conditions in the region, the nature of the VCS and its relationship with the state was different from that of its counterparts in Britain in important ways. Generally, social policy in areas such as taxation, social care, health and social security had been broadly similar to the rest of the UK (Acheson, 2010). However, there was a fear among successive direct-rule administrators that economic crisis would lead to more political violence (see Dixon, 2001, 361), and this led to NI being spared the worst of the Thatcherite neoliberal agenda being rolled out in other regions (Coulter, 2019, 128). As a result, NI would continue to experience relatively high levels of public expenditure and public-sector employment (Acheson et al, 2005, 198). Over the decades of direct rule, there also emerged a baffling technocracy of quangos and public bodies as civil servants and the British government sought to deliver public services in a relatively uncontroversial way (Carmichael and Knox, 2005, 782). This form of direct-rule administration, and the reliance on well-resourced but unaccountable quangos (Pinkerton and Campbell, 2002, 728), produced a 'sharply attenuated form of democracy' in the region (Carmichael, 2002, 27).

In such circumstances, decision-makers sought some way to both legitimise the policymaking process (Carmichael and Knox, 2004, 614; Hodgett, 2008, 168) and maintain some level of contact with the governed (Morrow, 1996). Turning to community-governance and civic-partnerships arrangements (Carmichael and Knox, 2004, 614), the civil service developed an extensive web of relationships with elements within civil society, including the VCS (Acheson, 2009, 70). Over the decades, what was supposed to be a temporary period of direct rule 'matured into "permanent impermanence"' (Carmichael and Knox, 2005, 772), and the VCS's recruitment into various service delivery arrangements and state-sector partnerships (Acheson et al, 2005, 198) meant that it began to occupy space 'which is normally the preserve of conventional politics' (Williamson et al, 2000, 51). The VCS became one of the beneficiaries of an overtly technocratic and Keynesian system of public administration and conflict management, and over time, close relationships developed between voluntary-sector elites and policymakers (McCall and Williamson, 2001, 364) as they became part of the 'shared endeavour of maintaining sufficient stability for public administration to continue to function' (Acheson, 2009, 70). Indeed, when funding from European Union programmes became available in the 1990s, the European Commission engaged directly with the VCS in the design of the programmes (Acheson 2009, 70), thus further consolidating a role for the VCS in local governance that would be 'unusual, if not unknown, elsewhere' (McCall and Williamson, 2001, 364).

As noted previously, much of the VCS's activities were embedded in the working-class communities most affected by the conflict, with activists responding to emerging needs and sectarian conflict and tensions at the local level (Kilmurray, 2017, 43). However, it was relatively uncommon for civil-society activity to emerge out of class-based solidarity across the political divide, and given the fact that government was seeking out 'respectable partners' that could add some legitimacy to the policymaking process, there was always a sense that a significant proportion of civil-society activity had its roots in a middle-class population that was 'historically immune from the vast majority of the violence that occurred in working-class districts' (Nagle, 2009, 188). With a continual absence of political progress, over time the VCS consolidated its role as a respectable and consulted partner of government, and with the exceptionalising discourses of 'tolerance', 'democratic accountability' and 'values' that surrounded the VCS, a culture developed where it was difficult to critique the actions of VCS organisations in any discussions concerning governance in NI (McAreavey, 2017, 166).

As Cochrane (2000, 11) explains, the quango model and the removal of power and responsibility from local political parties prompted a 'brain drain' within the political class during the period of direct rule, with much of the 'talent' using business or the voluntary sector as 'alternative avenues for making a positive contribution to their communities'. In a context in which VCS organisations had developed a formalised and institutionalised role, and with generous top-down support for a myriad of bureaucratic partnerships, consultative forums and 'network-facilitating' infrastructure organisations, the VCS increasingly came to be perceived by the credentialed middle-class as another site for building a career, and individuals would move back and forth from positions in the VCS and the public sector. In essence, the VCS was heavily subsidised by the British government and other actors in order to create a site for employment opportunities and the facilitation of government–civil society partnership and consultation, and direct-rule administrators hoped the VCS could become a space where cross-community interaction would be promoted and facilitated. With government's policy discourses and subsidies positioning the VCS to play specified roles, and with the sector being a key partner of government in public administration and welfare, it was not always clear to what extent the VCS's role was independent of government or just how collaborative the purportedly 'collaborative partnerships' were in practice (Hodgett and Johnson, 2001, 329; Acheson, 2009, 69). During periods of high unemployment or welfare and service cuts, some sections of the VCS continued to take antagonistic and campaigning approaches amid calls for 'working-class solidarity' (Kilmurray, 2017, 127), but the more direct political tactics that are sometimes associated with VCS groups were being actively discouraged by the VCS's patrons (Couto, 2001, 224).

It is important to note that during the decades of the Troubles there were some other regionally distinctive processes playing out in relation to VCS activity and the VCS's relationship with the state. Community organisations were sometimes seen by government as potential partners of paramilitary organisations (Acheson and Milofsky, 2008), and during the 1980s a policy of 'political vetting' was used by the British government to deny funding to organisations that were perceived to have close links with the non-state armed groups (Acheson, 2009, 70). In a context in which some unionist councils were already 'antagonistic towards Catholic community groups' (Birrell and Williamson, 2001, 207), the British government sought to drive a wedge between republicans and their support base in the community, and therefore it channelled large sums of money for temporary programmes into churches and church-run organisations (Acheson, 2009, 70).

Though there were regeneration programmes that focused on deprived urban areas (Kilmurray, 2017, 13), this vetting policy tended to impact the community infrastructure in the poorest (and mainly nationalist) communities, with funding flowing to what government regarded as 'respectable organisations' (Birrell and Williamson, 2001, 207). Given the dynamics of the conflict, British policies that were purportedly based on 'security' concerns tended to impact more on the nationalist community, but at the same time, they also had to manage the perceptions of the domestic and international audience (Dixon, 2009, 460) and give the impression that they were being 'even handed'. For example, in the earliest years of the conflict, Westminster had agreed to let Stormont introduce internment, but it was reported that the British Home Secretary had told the NI Prime Minister to 'lift some protestants if you can' for reasons of 'public relations' (McKittrick and McVea, 2012, 80; Fenton, 2018, 20). Similarly, when the vetting policy was implemented, individuals in the VCS noted that while it was primarily directed against the nationalist/republican community in areas such as West Belfast (see Birrell and Williamson, 2001, 207), funding was also withdrawn from a 'token number' of community programmes in unionist areas in order to 'to take the bad look off things' (Kilmurray, 2017, 144). However, in what was a clear illustration of the 'bottom line on independence' (Acheson, 2009, 78) for the VCS at the time, the vetting policy drew a very hostile response from a coalition of sectoral organisations (Acheson, 2009, 78; Kilmurray, 2017, 144).

By the early 1990s the direct-rule administration had 'allowed its policy of vetting to fall into disuse' (Birrell and Williamson, 2001, 207) as government increasingly came to see the VCS and community development as tools for achieving a range of political and social goals (Acheson and Milofsky, 2008), and a dormant community-relations infrastructure had been refreshed through the establishment of new institutions such as the Community Relations Council (Hughes and Carmichael, 1998). Much of the VCS remained largely embedded within the two main ethno-religious communities (Acheson, 2009; Acheson, 2013), but as outlined here, it was consistently seen by direct-rule governments as having value as a partner in the drive towards a more peaceful and economically and socially stable NI. Throughout the 1990s, government strategies and network and institution-building efforts continued to reflect this belief, and as Acheson (2010, 177) has outlined, the direct-rule period was characterised by various 'covert and not so covert attempts to recruit elements of civil society' to the tasks of conflict management and the building of greater civic engagement with the state.

With additional support from the EU and international funders, the VCS became a key partner in urban regeneration, economic development, employment and anti-poverty initiatives (Hodgett and Johnson, 2001; McCall and Williamson, 2001; Kilmurray, 2017), and in the absence of a local parliament, the VCS was increasingly filling the political vacuum by becoming a kind of 'proto-representative' forum (Birrell and Williamson, 2001, 207). There was further development of the infrastructure for rural voluntary and community activity (see Acheson et al, 2004, 57), and more of a focus within government agencies on using community development approaches as a way of including 'new groups in the policy-formation process' (Hodgett, 2008, 175). UK-wide reviews of the VCS initiated in Westminster further consolidated the role of the VCS in Northern Irish society, for they set in motion policy processes that would eventually lead 'to a regional strategy for the support of the voluntary sector and of community development' (Acheson et al, 2005, 198). In the rest of the UK, these types of reviews were often concerned with efficiency and how the VCS could deliver government service-delivery contracts (see Lewis, 1999). In comparison, in NI there was more of a focus on the VCS's unique role in the particular social and political circumstances of the region and on the role of community development (Acheson, 1995). Government also established a Voluntary Activity Unit to manage government–VCS relationships and provide 'a focus for Government's policies toward the voluntary and community sector' (Birrell and Williamson. 2001, 209).

The shift to peace and neoliberalism

In the wake of the paramilitary ceasefires and the 1998 GFA, the VCS experienced another period of 'rapid growth' (McCall and Williamson, 2001, 364) due to funding from EU peace programmes (McCall and O'Dowd, 2008, 30), government and private foundations (Braniff and Byrne, 2014, 54). With the arrival of the Labour government in 1997 and their third-way approach to welfare (Fyfe, 2005), their desire to build social capital (Imrie and Raco, 2003, 26) and their celebration of active citizenship, community and civil society (Levitas, 2000; Fyfe, 2005), the VCS was also the beneficiary of a new UK-wide wave of partnership, network building and civil-society boosterism. This was a time of broader UK and EU interest in the 'concepts of civil society, third way politics, and the use of the nonprofit sector for contracted service delivery' (O'Regan, 2001, 250), and it was a period that saw the further development of a general 'network governance milieu' (Davies, 2011a, 9). Within this milieu, there was an emphasis on harnessing the talents and contributions of multiple agencies in service delivery and decision-making processes (see Blair, 1999, in Alcock and Kendall, 2010, 6), and influenced by the work of authors such as Putnam (2000), third-wayist policy narratives celebrated the role and virtues of apolitical civil-society organisations and the notion that partnership and capacity-building could unlock unrealised social resources within communities (Kearns, 2003). Throughout this period, the British government in NI and local administrators, just like governments and transnational organisations around the world (Davies, 2012b, 3), often seemed to be suggesting that they must network with citizens and civil society groups if they were to 'get anything done'. Given the history of governance in the region and the role played by its VCS,

NI would prove to be fertile ground for a communitarian third-way discourse, network governance ideas and the European Commission's celebration of voluntary organisations. In such an environment, it is unsurprising that there should be a peace dividend for the VCS, with government and external funders resourcing a peace industry made up of networks and partnerships involving the VCS, governmental and non-governmental funders and the private sector (see Kearney and Williamson, 2001; Shirlow and Murtagh, 2004; Acheson and Milofsky, 2008; McCall and O'Dowd, 2008; Braniff and Byrne, 2014).

The EU peace programmes and statutory and other international sources have also allocated monies to groups working with politically motivated ex-prisoners. These groups have been involved in demilitarising their local communities, restorative-justice programmes (Kilmurray, 2017), removing or replacing paramilitary flags and murals, diffusing interface tensions (Mitchell, 2008, 8) and engagement exercises with former adversaries across the republican/loyalist divide (Shirlow et al, 2005). Over the decades, there has been some discussion about the role in the VCS of former political prisoners, ex-combatants and 'community gatekeepers' vis-à-vis the role of established 'safe hands' (Kilmurray, 2017, 272). In the wake of the ceasefires and GFA, and in the absence of a clearly articulated disarmament, demobilisation and reintegration strategy for ex-combatants (McEvoy and Shirlow 2009, 33), paramilitaries' 'acquiescence to the peace process' was helped by the fact that funding from various sources facilitated their 'takeover of salaried roles in the grassroots peacebuilding sector' (Holland and Rabrenovic, 2018, 734).[2] While the signing of the peace accord may have heralded an era of 'post-conflict' in NI, research suggests that the region has struggled to fully reintegrate ex-combatants from state and non-state forces into peace-time society, with disarmament and demilitarisation taking precedence over genuine demobilisation and integration (Rolston, 2007). While many of the ex-prisoner 'self-help' organisations provide essential services to what are often a vulnerable and marginalised section of NI's post-conflict society (Shirlow and Hughes, 2014), the role of ex-combatants in the wider community sector meant that the term 'community worker' became 'synonymous for many with the term paramilitary' (McKinney, 2017) and raised difficult questions about local power structures and 'community gatekeepers'.

In the NI peace process, civil society would become a synonym for the good society – a sphere of society characterised by positive norms and values, responsible citizenship and 'a repository of tolerance, non-discrimination, non-violence, trust and cooperation, freedom and democracy' (Coakley and O'Dowd, 2007, 21). Rather than such discourses capturing the reality of civil-society institutions that both reflected and constituted the region's social divisions, they were more likely reflective of broader political goals and elite concerns. Political elites will have been conscious of the fact that, up until the time the agreement was given popular consent and legitimacy through a referendum, the negotiation of the accord was a largely secretive and elite-driven affair (Nagle, 2018, 399), with civil society (in the broadest sense) being largely spectators. They would also have been conscious of the fact that within a few years of its signing, there was a 'deepening of the agreement's legitimacy crisis among NI's Protestants' (MacGinty, 2004), with the unionist community 'deeply divided along pro- and anti-Agreement lines' (McCall and Williamson, 2001, 364). Hence, in a continuation of longstanding British policy (see Dixon, 1997, 2), it made sense that Westminster would seek to undergird the agreement with more 'bottom-up' measures enacted by dependent civil-society institutions. As we have already seen, the VCS had long facilitated 'forums for communication and dialogue when no others existed in the formal political arena' (Cochrane, 2000, 19), and there was no reason why this sectoral experience could not be utilised in efforts to prop up the fledgling peace.

The nature and role of the VCS can only really be understood in the context of the political economy, policies and dominant discourses that have emerged in the post-ceasefire and post-accord era. As Coulter (2019, 124) outlines, the champions of the GFA recognised that there was a need to turn around the region's 'long ailing economy', and in selling the agreement to the NI electorate, they argued that the accord was not just a vote for peace but also a vote for stability and prosperity (see Blair, 1998, in Coulter, 2019, 124; Coulter, 2014). The end of the worst of the conflict led to the promise of a broad-based 'peace dividend' (Knox, 2014), and as NI could begin to tap into reserves of international goodwill towards the region, there was a hope of increased inward investment (Coulter, 2019, 124). In the wake of the GFA, there was an understandable expectation that the resources expended on security could be used for infrastructural development and public services (Horgan, 2006, 661). However, in the decades following the agreement, NI would undergo a 'double transition' to both peace and neoliberalism (McCabe, 2013, 4), with decision makers committing NI to property-based and market-driven economic development and urban regeneration that promised 'trickle-down' benefits for working-class communities (see Murtagh 2011; Murtagh and Shirlow, 2012; Coyles, 2013; O'Dowd and Komarova 2013; Boland et al, 2017).

Reflecting the influence of 'the architects of the peace process in Washington and London' (Kelly, 2012, 2), neoliberal economic ideas came to have a profound impact on the political and economic 'common sense' in NI. Under the banner of 'rebalancing the economy', all the major parties would acquiesce to or espouse (Horgan and Gray, 2012, 467) a neoliberal mix of tax cuts, public-sector cuts, privatisation, consumerism, private-sector-led 'regeneration', 'flexible' labour arrangements and 'competitive' wages (Horgan and Gray, 2012; Kelly, 2012; Baker, 2014; Coulter, 2019). Given the fact that decision makers had to contend with a complex array of entrenched social, political and economic forces, processes and structures left over from the conflict, the region's neoliberal agenda did not reflect 'a unified ideology and set of practices' (Nagle, 2009, 174). Rather, among decision makers, there was a general tilt towards embracing the idea that neoliberalism, consumerism and economic growth had 'conflict-solving powers' (Hillyard et al, 2005, 47; Kelly, 2012; Barry, 2019, 40). In addition, the first devolved coalition government, with its emphasis on cross-party agreement, was characterised by a 'lowest common denominator' form of policymaking (McLaughlin, 2005, 116), with conservative and risk-averse policies benefiting only 'the unambiguously deserving poor, including children and older people' (Gray and Birrell, 2011, 14). Though there was to be little evidence of a peace dividend in some of the poorer communities that had suffered the worst consequences of the conflict (O'Hearn, 2008; Knox, 2014; Ferguson and Halliday, 2020), criticism of the region's policy direction was muted by the fact that the 'double transition' to peace and neoliberalism (McCabe, 2013, 4) was accompanied by a 'moralising and often finger-wagging' discourse (Barry, 2019, 40). This 'spoiler' narrative framed Left-leaning critiques of Stormont's decisions as attempts to undermine the peace process (Hearty, 2018, 133; Barry, 2019, 406), and in this climate, it made sense for resource-dependent civil society actors to perform as if government and the VCS were 'social partners', with all 'pulling in the same direction' to deliver on an agreed and shared vision for NI (see DSD, 2011).

Indeed, a VCS that was dependent on UK government and European Commission funds in order to resource 'formal and professionalized structures' (Acheson and Milofsky, 2008, 76) could play a key role in the roll out of this neoliberal agenda. As Davies (2009a, 88; 2011, 47; 2012a, 2696) has illustrated, advocates of neoliberalism can attempt to embed a benign cooperativeness in society in order to deliver the social stability that is necessary for a deregulated market economy to function, and a central part of the neoliberal project is the creation of conditions whereby subordinate groups (or those who claim to speak on their behalf) will reject conflict for 'the virtues' of a 'partnership ethos' of cooperativeness, pragmatism and consensus. By utilising funding dependency to secure sectoral buy-in to policy discourses that proclaimed the value of 'community', apolitical voluntary activity, partnership, cooperation, networking and social capital, the VCS could help in the delivery and maintenance of social and political stability at the local level through its work in 'single-identity' community development and cross-community peace programmes. Therefore, essential as this work might be from a peace-building perspective, it also brought added value when looked at through a neoliberal frame. In addition, while power would remain at 'the centre', the responsibility for managing some of the worst consequences of the conflict and the fallout from a neoliberal policy agenda could be transferred away from the state and down to the community level, and potential critics of the policy agenda will have been silenced by funding dependency and powerful discourses that defined the norms of acceptable behaviour within government's partnership spaces (see Davies, 2011a).

Following the GFA, the VCS had to shift its focus onto building relationships with local parties and politicians. These are the same parties and politicians who, when 'neutered' by direct rule, had become 'jealous and frustrated by the success of the sector' (McCall and Williamson, 2001, 364) and its usurpation of 'the proper functions of elected representatives' (McCall and O'Dowd, 2008, 33). The Programmes for Government of devolved administrations allayed any fears about conflict and antagonism between local politicians and the VCS, and the devolved administrations continued to echo the rhetoric of direct-rule administrations by suggesting that it is important to involve the VCS in policies and programs aimed at strengthening 'community wellbeing' (Acheson, 2010, 184). In line with the civil-society boosterism that was characteristic of the time, the Joint Government Voluntary and Community Sector Forum was established in 1998 and, despite resistance from some politicians, relationships with government and civil society were further formalised with the establishment of the Civic Forum (McCall and Williamson, 2001, 363). The broader-based Civic Forum is now defunct, and in many respects it was simply a creature of New Labour rhetoric about 'public participation in the policy process' (McCall and Williamson, 2001). As was the case in NI, elected politicians have tended to reject the notion that there is a gap between them and the electorate that needs to be filled, and therefore they can be reluctant to fund or support such spaces (Nolan and Wilson, 2015). With an ill-defined remit, a fragmented membership of the unelected and unelectable (Adshead and Tonge, 2009) and a limited budget, this particular forum was unlikely to survive the hostility it faced from (mainly) unionist politicians.

When the power-sharing Assembly was suspended in 2002, the Blair government extended the 'palpably neoliberal strategies that had been introduced throughout the rest of the United Kingdom' (Coulter, 2019, 129) to NI, and direct-rule ministers sought to streamline public administration and tilt policies in the direction of privatisation (Acheson, 2010, 179). NI's equivalents of area-based programs such as neighbourhood renewal emphasised the need to build the 'social fabric' (Murtagh et al, 2008, 44), and the VCS played a role within a slew of partnerships, networks and forums (Greer, 2001; Acheson and Milofsky, 2008; Muir, 2010; Murtagh and Shirlow, 2012). Like their UK counterparts, the myriad of area-based programmes and other civil society–government partnerships drew on the language of social capital, collaboration, social networks and community revival (CRU, 2005; DSD, 2006; Muir, 2011). As Hodgett and Johnson (2001, 331) have suggested, the VCS has a long history of involvement in place-based regeneration partnerships that had 'ostensibly neoliberal theoretical origins', but due to the unique political circumstances and governance arrangements of NI there has been a tendency for such programmes to be given a local twist through the influence of the EU and processes of 'indigenous policy evolution'. More recent place-based regeneration efforts can be seen as a continuation of this trend, with political and civil-society actors working in local partnerships centred around the themes of regeneration and development, but also peace and reconciliation (Acheson and Milofsky, 2008). In addition, a strategic framework for community relations was introduced by the British government in the absence of the local assembly (Campbell et al, 2008, 23). This strategy suggested that the VCS had made a 'powerful contribution to the achievement of better relations between communities', and therefore it would continue to play a central role in future 'good relations' efforts (CRU, 2005, 54). However, just as in other regions, a 'contract culture' was to become more embedded during this New Labour direct-rule interregnum (Acheson, 2013, 10), and the VCS in NI faced the same issues over independence, state co-option, top-down regulation, bureaucracy and isomorphism as its UK counterparts (Ketola and Hughes, 2018).

After the assembly was restored in 2007, the new administration was dominated by Sinn Féin and the Democratic Unionist Party. The two parties continued to promote the 'neoliberal order' that had become so central to NI's project of 'economic renaissance', though simultaneously they also deployed a 'populist rhetoric that articulates welfare protection and social mobility' (Murtagh and Shirlow, 2012, 47). More recently, the Executive had sought the power to reduce NI's corporation tax rate and has explored other measures that would make the region more 'competitive', but as Murtagh (2018, 444) explains, the impact of such fiscal changes on 'communities with few assets, skills and educational underperformance is rarely articulated with any conviction'. This administration also reiterated government's commitment to act collaboratively with partners in the VCS, and despite austerity-driven cutbacks, the organised bureaucracy of the voluntary and community industry would continue to enjoy generous funding from government departments. A concordat between the voluntary sector and government was agreed by political and voluntary-sector representatives in 2011 (hereafter 'the concordat'). This document describes how partnership arrangements between the VCS and government were mechanisms that 'would assist citizens and communities to empower themselves' and in the process, 'make a significant contribution to democratic governance' (DSD, 2011, 2). However, in line with trends across the UK, it became increasingly clear that the VCS only had value so far as it could deliver public services in an efficient manner and to a 'predetermined script', and missing from this new script was the references to the VCS's role in peacebuilding (Acheson, 2013, 10). This rhetoric about civil society and grassroots peacebuilding helped to provide many organisations with a discourse that justified their existence (and the funding that paid for this existence), and as NI slowly dropped off the radar of some international funders and philanthropists, the VCS was somewhat robbed of the top-down rhetorical support that gave weight to the claim that it was a distinctive and transformative agent in Northern Irish society (Acheson, 2013, 8).

Conclusion

Despite the decades of close government–VCS relationships and the sector's central role in governance, and despite the co-option and dependency that occurred during the conflict and the New Labour years, government has continued to be a cheerleader in the representation of the VCS as strong, critical, campaigning and independent (DSD, 2011). However, with a clear move away from the civil-society boosterism of the peace-process era, recent consultations and 'toolkits' suggest a subtle shift in tone in government's rhetoric concerning its relationship with the VCS. These documents contain rhetorical artefacts from the 'golden age' of the New Labour era, with government claiming that it wants to support and 'harness the energy and social capital which exists in communities' (DfC, 2016, 3). However, in language that is strikingly similar to that employed by Conservative government ministers, this policy documentation also argues that the VCS must become more sustainable and transition 'away from reliance on grant based funding' (DfC, 2016, 3). NI's government departments are now seeking to help third sector organisations develop the skills and knowledge they will need to 'raise investment', access a more diverse range of income sources and to survive the 'significant challenges in relation to a much tighter public funding environment' (DfC, 2016, 4).

THREE

Getting connected: celebrating the value of connections and networks

As the previous chapter suggested, at various times in the region's history, efforts have been made to 'mainstream' the role of the VCS in Northern Irish society and governance. This chapter maps out some of the networks, partnerships and spaces that emerged out of a succession of initiatives that sought to reimagine relationships within and between the VCS and government, and it explores interviewees' experiences of participating in multi-actor networks, partnerships and processes of relationship building. In doing so, we explore how and why networks and partnerships come into existence, the politics and economics of partnership and relationship building, and the behaviours, dispositions, norms and values that create and sustain formal and informal partnerships, networks and relationships. We also sketch out the ways in which multi-actor networks continue to be an important part of the various strategies for managing the region's social and political divisions and the issues associated with its transition from conflict to relative peace. In this chapter, we will see how individuals operating in seemingly distinct spheres and sectors often describe networking, relationship building and partnership in similar ways, and how they often reach for the same phrases and concepts to describe networking practices and outcomes. As will become clear, the narratives put forward by many interviewees are strikingly similar to the orthodox and positive-sum narratives of multi-actor and multi-level partnership that have been put forward by UK governments, transnational institutions, voices from within the VCS, local administrators and some strands of scholarship. In later chapters, we will begin to critically unpack these more optimistic narratives.

The value of horizontal networks at the community level

As the data in this chapter will demonstrate, VCS organisations operate within a complex, contingent and changeable ecosystem that is made up of various and varied organisations, formal partnerships, contractual relationships and informal networks. Sitting alongside the wide range of locally based community development organisations (CDOs), there are sectoral service providers operating in a variety of thematic policy areas and at different geographical scales; a wider bureaucracy of infrastructural agencies and umbrella organisations that support the VCS as a whole or some of its thematic subsectors; grant-making agencies, foundations, partnership boards and quangos; formalised spaces for government–VCS interaction; and a complex web of formal and informal relationships involving the VCS, funders, consultants, the private sector and academic researchers. This web of relationships and networks inevitably reflects some of the historical events, policy priorities and funding practices outlined in the previous chapters. However, it is also reflective of specific ideological influences on policymaking and policymakers, and the common assumption that the VCS and government are both attempting to address complex issues that require multi-agency responses. The following sections explore the formal and informal networks community organisations are a part of, and the nature of some of their work at the local level.

Making the connections

In surveys of organisations in the VCS, 'community development' tops the list in terms of the 'main areas of work' that organisations claim to be engaged in (NICVA, 2016). For a number of interviewees from the community sector, small and medium-sized community-based organisations have an embeddedness within the community and an ability to deliver for 'hard to reach' groups and communities. This embeddedness and reach into the community would, for some interviewees, be difficult for a governmental agency to emulate.

> 'What we [community organisations] excel at is an ability to reach people the government can't reach. If you want to get into the heart of North Belfast or Derry or rural areas or disadvantaged areas, you are only going to be able to do that through a community organisation.' (Interviewee from a VCS organisation; hereafter VCS)

Alongside delivering a range of services at the community level and acting as a site for community interaction, community development agencies often see the building and strengthening of horizontal and vertical relationships and networks as a core part of their mission.[1]

Similarly, as part of its community capacity-building programmes, government has sought to strengthen relationships among groups involved in community development projects. As one community development worker (CDW) explains, a healthy civil society and cohesive community will value connectivity at the grassroots level, and those involved in on-the-ground activity must value external connections and look outside the immediate community for linkages and partners.

> 'To have an active civic society you need a lot of grassroots and a lot of community connections, they are all very important for community cohesion … organisations can't be only asking about services for the community. They need to ask themselves "what can we do to deliver services for the community?" … They need to ask themselves, "what can we do for our communities and who are we in partnership with to deliver these services?"' (VCS)

Community organisations often actively seek out partners in their efforts to get things done, and in doing so, they can form a web of grassroots and vertical connections. Relationships can develop organically between organisations, or they may develop when organisations come together to work on funded projects. These horizontal relationships can be sustained by a common ethos of community development and mutual respect, even when there exists differences in terms of organisational cultures and visions for the future. As one CDW explains:

> 'Sometimes we will come together to deliver work in partnership … to a great extent we all come from the same ethos of community development and we all have visions of where we want to be, they might be different, but we respect each other.' (VCS)

It is important to note the difficult context within which this relationship building is taking place. The historical division between the communities has meant that building relationships can be far from easy. In such circumstances, evidence of good working relationships between community groups should not be used to promote a false sense of positivity when so many legacies of the conflict remain unresolved.

> 'Don't underestimate how difficult the legacy of the past makes it [building relationships] … we don't want to promote a false sense of positivity … the reality is, there is a lot of hangover from the past and a lot of legacy going on in all of our communities.' (VCS)

Despite the legacy issues playing out on the ground, some CDO interviewees stress that an instinct for building relationships brings disparate groups together in formal partnerships and informal networks. This ethos of partnership and relationship building reflects the long history of CDOs working together to develop inter-community ways of alleviating conflict, mistrust and tensions, and the long history of organisations working across the political divide on issues of shared concern (Kilmurray, 2017, 43; Hancock, 2019, 7).[2] Network building develops and sustains relationships that allow for the exchange of information among the infrastructure of organised institutions and agencies in the area.

> 'Locally, most organisations would have some connection with us ... that can be sometimes quite difficult depending on the "small–p" politics, but we have developed very good relationships ... locally, it's really about maintaining relationships and making sure, within reason, everybody knows everybody and what's going on.' (VCS)

The work involved in maintaining informal information-sharing networks is seen as additional to the funded project work of the community groups. In fact, according to some interviewees, much of the informal relationship-building efforts go unfunded. In an example of the VCS's 'added value', it is not top-down initiatives and funding that sustain cross-community and inter-organisational networks and relationships, but rather trust and necessity.

> 'Nobody funds that [informal] work, but you need that, and that takes trust.' (VCS)

One CDO interviewee with an ex-combatant background is keen to stress the need for this kind of 'bottom-up' approach to community development, pointing to how this localised relationship building provides the groundwork for more ambitious goals:

> 'Where does it all start? Bottom up. It's what gets built at the grassroots, the local infrastructure, the local relationships. First and foremost, that takes good working relationships between the representatives of each community.' (VCS)

This interviewee suggests that CDWs act as 'representatives' of communities when they meet each other across the communal divide,[3] and that the relationships they have forged can become gateways through which the two communities can begin to interact. In line with government community-relations strategies, this interviewee wants to see the 'normalisation' of relationships within civil society. This normalisation can be driven by the creation of opportunities for participation, contact, interaction and the building of social capital, and the VCS can facilitate these opportunities. As the same interviewee explains:

'We learnt long ago it wasn't about community workers meeting each other ... that doesn't build relations within a community, that builds relations between two people that represent the community. It's not about gatekeeping, it's about being gateways. It's about trickling them relationships into communities and making them normalised relations, giving local people the chance and ability and confidence to begin to interact. We run events that are a chance to bring people together, create a social capital, create improved relations, and lower the tensions.' (VCS)

In a theme that is common among many working in community development, one CDW from a republican working-class area suggests that a focus on interests and issues that cut across traditional political cleavages is a major factor in making local horizontal partnerships and networks work.

'A lot of emphasis is put on our differences ... but we put a big emphasis on what do we have in common, and that's what is lost in the wash sometimes ... we say the empty plate in the loyalist community is the same as the empty plate in the republican community.' (VCS)

In deeply segregated areas, and in an environment where sporadic violence causes fear and mistrust, networks survive because people have confidence that those on the other side of the interface will keep to their word and deliver on their commitments. Confidence in others, and past collaborative successes, allows networked actors to build on their achievements and continuously strengthen and develop local partnerships and relationships. As the same CDW explains:

'People around here, when they give their word on something, they deliver. They do their best to deliver ... that's my view of the loyalists I work with ... every year [our work] is at a different stage of development and partnership building and relationship building.' (VCS)

If there is one idea that seems to drive the networking practices of VCS groups, it is the notion that the issues they are dealing with are complex, and that their work is most effective as part of wider 'joined-up' multi-agency responses. What is clear in much of the talk of the CDWs is that the local relationships they have built and maintained need to be 'plugged in' to wider networks. Partnerships and relationships, in their view, need to be developed with agencies and organisations from outside the community and from outside the VCS. Community development agencies have focused on building local connections, but at the same time, they have worked towards building relationships with infrastructure agencies, voluntary-sector partners and government agencies and departments.

'Local and focused approaches and local relationships deliver the best results, a bottom-up approach. At the end of the day, it is about community endorsement; at the end of the day, it's about participation and empowerment. But that needs middle support and top-down backing. I would work with a lot of statutory agencies in my practice.' (VCS)

In the NI context, some of the most complex of problems are often associated with the region's political divisions and the legacies of the conflict. For example, CDWs explain how their areas can experience periodic increases in sectarian tensions. When this occurs, the 'chill factors' of territorial politics may come back into play, with the flying of flags and attempts to label territory as belonging to one community. In some cases, areas may also experience sporadic low-level violence between the two communities. The position of the professional CDWs allows them to draw on the relationships they have developed with each other, with government agencies and paramilitaries to negotiate local agreements on flags and emblems or negotiate their removal. This is just one example of the CDW's role being akin to that of the 'everyday fixer' as identified by Hendriks and Tops (2005, 475), with the CDW acting as a conduit between state agencies, residents and other powerful groups in the community to deal with problems and complaints as they arise. In attempts to manage flare ups of violence at community interfaces, and in developing strategies for dealing with other community safety issues, CDOs developed horizontal relationships across the divide, but also vertical relationships with individuals and agencies that are external to the VCS, such as politicians, businesses, the police and government agencies.

> 'The procedure was that we spoke to politicians ... they organised the meetings initially to see what we could do to have it [the violence] quelled here. We met the management teams [of the local businesses] ... we met the police ... a whole group of people have come together, including residents, community workers, police, housing executive [to design and deliver strategies].' (VCS)

Cooperation across distinct community interfaces, and across gradients of power and authority, also led to initiatives that would increase the mobility of working-class communities and help facilitate their inclusion into the mainstream of Northern Irish society. As one CDW working in a deeply segregated area explains:

> 'We have seen community development open up peace lines and gates to increase people's mobility. We have seen it create a social capital, create relationships on a cross-community basis that allows that to occur and increase. It's that social capital that can give way to an economic baseline ... it makes them [people in the community] a stakeholder in society, being able to participate in civic, economic and social life is what improves people's quality of life. Working with statutory agencies are a massive part of those relationships.' (VCS)

It seems that the outcome of vertical and horizontal networking at the local level is practical action on some of the more 'wicked problems' affecting communities. In some areas, the CDWs' efforts appear to be concrete examples of government's concordat commitments to 'joined-up activity' between government and the VCS (DSD, 2011, 8). The financial resources made available to the VCS, the legitimacy and access that came from the professionalisation of the VCS, and the proximity of decision makers in the wake of the peace process and devolution, seem to have allowed community activists to build links and networks with decision makers as well as statutory and other agencies. The interviewees' experiences are also reminiscent of policy discourses concerning ideas about 'empowering those closest to problems', and call to mind government commitments to working with and consulting those with the most knowledge of the causes of social issues. In the language of the New Labour policy agendas that informed community development and government–VCS relationships in the years after the GFA, the networking examples outlined by the interviewees can be seen as bridging and linking social capital in action. The networks and their successes can be seen as the fruition of a longstanding commitment to an inclusive 'partnership agenda' in government, and as the outcome of the decades-long financial and moral support that government and external funders have given to the VCS. The CDOs' expertise and value, as another CDW explains, has now been recognised by decision makers:

> 'All of the politicians have made a kind of quiet commitment to the community organisations because they recognise their value.' (VCS)

Building and strengthening 'the fabric of society'

Alongside the CDOs sits a range of service providers, a wider bureaucracy of infrastructural agencies and umbrella organisations, grant-making trusts and funders. Given the complex web of relationships and sectoral interdependencies that make up the VCS ecosystem, it was also important to capture the views of interviewees from these larger or more regional organisations on local relationship building and community development. Resonant of the social capital and 'self help' policy discourses of recent decades, for many interviewees from within this wider VCS bureaucracy, the VCS at the local level can be the driving force behind the development of trusting relationships between neighbours, and it is often seen as building and sustaining relations of 'good neighbourliness'. The VCS, in the form of CDOs that are embedded within a geographic community or community of interest, promote a sense of confidence, encourage a spirit of self-help and empower often-marginalised individuals to take control over their own lives and influence the decisions that affect them. For many interviewees that work in larger organisations, grant-making and infrastructure bodies and service-delivery agencies, it is important to protect and maintain those organisations that "make up the fabric" of society.

> 'Community organisations can do the things the state isn't going to do and a lot of that I think is in that area that would be formative in terms of social capital … if the area was getting run down they would be saying what we can do to improve it? … people will be saying "I like living here" … "you can depend on your neighbours" … there are lots of activities going on, people will have a good feeling about their area.' (VCS)

Interviewees from some larger organisations support the idea of sectoral diversity and suggest that smaller, locally based organisations should be able to compete for funding and contracts. These interviewees would often point out that they value the work of smaller organisations, they recognise the need for grant funding, and they acknowledge the expertise, knowledge and localism of these organisations in terms of delivering services for hard-to-reach groups. For some interviewees, there needs to be some push back against a government funding model that has overly privileged notions like 'value for money', for such a model cannot account for the added value and positive externalities that a grant to a VCS organisation brings. Again, at the heart of these arguments is the idea of investing in and stimulating the development of social capital, and the added value or 'spin offs' this may bring.

> 'There is a fashion in the public sector to use procurement and that's because they believe it to be the straightforward way to share out scarce resources ... they also believe that it gives the impression of looking for value for money ... I would oppose that ... government should be interested not just in the transaction, "what service will you deliver for me", it is also about the benefit you might see that organisation having in the community ... there is a bigger philosophical question around things like social capital ... you may well get a bigger return [from a grant] if you consider what the other spin offs might be.' (VCS)

Interviewees working within larger organisations and the wider sectoral bureaucracy argue that government funders could better formalise relationships and partnerships between smaller and larger organisations in their procurement processes, and they suggest that government officials must be 'sophisticated' in how they develop future relationships with different types and sizes of organisation. Just as with interviewees from community-based organisations, they argue that it is important that a localised community spirit and the social capital of a particular group or community fit within a wider system of networks and connections. Similar to interviewees from the purportedly more grassroots organisations, those from larger organisations draw on the idea that being 'connected' allows the collective voice of the community to be heard when decisions are being made that will affect community members' everyday lives. Communities, through their community groups, are seen to bring a richness and localised knowledge to decision making, in that they know what does and does not work. In this respect, sectoral views resonate with much of the social capital literature and the partnership and participatory 'turns' in policy discourses outlined in previous chapters. As an interviewee from one of the larger charities explains:

'If you have got an area and a district that is well connected and cohesive, they can make their voice heard … community development is about involving people in the decisions that affect their lives, because they will tell you [the decision makers] what hasn't worked, what their bugbears have been, and that gives you a chance to do something about that and address it.' (VCS)

Interviewees, from community organisations to the bureaucratic, funding and service-delivery infrastructure, often see the VCS as an important site for social-capital generation because of its vertical and horizontal networking capability. Its ability to build linkages, particularly across community cleavages, is seen as a central part of the story of the VCS's intangible 'added value'. As one VCS interviewee explains:

'What is this elusive added value [of the VCS]? A lot of it is about building relationships. Voluntary and community activity, yes, it's delivering services on behalf of the state, but there is something else … building relationships externally with those who are different from you, in a Northern Ireland context, in terms of religion obviously.' (VCS)

Building horizontal connections within and between communities is believed to be an important part of the work of the VCS, particularly in a divided society like NI. However, as with the interviewees from smaller community organisations, another part of the VCS's elusive added-value is the way it develops relationships across gradients of power. This allows for the articulation of the perspective and needs of marginalised and disadvantaged groups within policy and decision-making debates and discussions. Therefore, in order to have influence, in order to bring the 'richness' of the VCS's views to the table, communities and organisations must build linkages with those who have power and resources. As another VCS interviewee explains:

'Also, it's about developing relationships with those who have power and resources. There is this whole issue about power structures and how you actually connect those people who haven't got with those who have. This is what voluntary and community organisations can do, they can enhance the social capital of communities, they can enhance the social capital of disadvantaged client groups.' (VCS)

Why those with power and resources should wish to connect with subordinate groups, and why they would open their decision-making structures to these groups, is a complex question. Many of the interviewees seem to suggest that political and bureaucratic elites have come to recognise the VCS as the representatives of different communities of interest, and that decision makers have recognised the value of the sector's knowledge in putting together strategies 'that work'. Some interviewees, from both the VCS and government, would suggest that the voice of the VCS is listened to by decision makers, and that it has become part of the decision-making process due to its long experience as a partner in policy development, service delivery and regeneration networks. These networks are apparently characterised by a genuine co-dependency between VCS organisations and government, and sectoral organisations have become a credible voice through longstanding relationships and a clear ability to evidence results. There is also often an assumption that dominant and subordinate groups have shared interests, goals and hopes, and that the only potential disagreement is in the right way to achieve these goals. At other times, the community or group voice, articulated by the VCS, is seen as acting as a counterweight to the expert or professionalised discourses that could allow external agencies to do things to, rather than with, communities and service users. The voice of the community or clients can be articulated by the VCS as 'insiders' to governance and service delivery partnerships, or within government's 'invited spaces' and forums. Facilitated by investment from non-governmental and international funders in particular, organisations may also take a 'community participation' approach to their advocacy work, bringing communities from across the sectarian divide together to work on common issues and 'call large public bodies to account' in ways they may be not be accustomed to (Knox and Quirk, 2016, 215).

As we have already seen in previous sections, a very structural conceptualisation of social capital, one that draws heavily on ideas about networks and relationships (as opposed to norms and values), seems to have become a useful way for the VCS to articulate what it perceives itself as doing on an everyday basis. The VCS is often seen as having a generalised ability to accumulate connections, and these connections are believed to be a resource on which disadvantaged communities and groups can draw. Framing relationships and networks as a resource in and of themselves could be part of an effort to justify the bewildering array of governance networks, consultative forums and grant and contract-based 'partnerships'. Or, as some interviewees suggest, maybe it is the case that disadvantaged communities and client groups are empowered by networked relationships: they have access to those with power and resources and the network gives them a platform to make their voices heard. In theory, it is within that wider networked system that communities and service users can begin to rebalance the distribution of power and challenge the way resources are used and distributed. It is clear that ideas around collaboration and vertical and horizontal partnership and relationship building are central to sectoral practice, and they have become a key part of the narratives that surround the VCS and its relationship with government. This perceived need for a collaborative ethos is captured succinctly by one interviewee:

'No organisation can be responsible for meeting the needs of even its client group, so it is inevitable, and it is almost like a moral imperative, that organisations need to collaborate with others ... having a good ethos and values is looking at the needs of the communities and people you are serving and saying "who else do we need to be working with around that".' (VCS)

Developing the state–civil society partnership: vertical relationship building

Reflecting the region's long history of shared government–VCS enterprise, over the last few decades institutional arrangements that formalise linkages at the civil society–government interface have been developed. As well as spaces created by government, sectoral infrastructure organisations have historically hosted policy forums, conferences and departmental monitoring groups with the aim of enhancing the VCS's capacity to engage with the policymaking process (Birrel and Gormley-Heenan, 2015, 216). Government's non-departmental public bodies have established permanent forums (Birrel and Gormley-Heenan, 2015, 216) and networks in order to involve residents, service users and community associations in discussing and developing services. Intra-sectoral and government–civil society collaboration has allowed for the creation of participatory networks that bring together individuals with shared interests (for example, children and young people, service users or victims and survivors) to discuss their issues and communicate their concerns to government. We can see from the data presented that this trend has continued, with more and more mechanisms being created to facilitate formal and informal vertical networking between VCS organisations and government agencies. Distinctive spaces for government–VCS interaction have been carved out, with these spaces becoming physical manifestations of government's rhetorical recognition of the VCS's value and knowledge, and its 'special relationship' with government. As one government official explains:

> 'There is a special relationship between the voluntary and community sector and government ... every government department should be, in their relationship with the voluntary and community sector, they should be treating them equitably and with respect and in accordance with the values and principles as espoused in the concordat.' (Government official)

The evidence of a mass of spaces for engagement and partnership between the VCS and government would suggest that the VCS is correct in assuming that the governing bureaucracy recognises the value of the sector's voice in decision-making processes and implementation. The VCS is seen as a legitimate voice in policy debates, and as one government official explains, when the VCS and government interact, officials 'are speaking to them as advocates for the people they are representing'. This governmental recognition of the special role of the VCS, and recognition of its special relationship with government, shows no sign of waning. The agreement that resurrected the devolved institutions in 2020 was focused on complex and disputed issues around institutional mechanisms within the assembly, Brexit, culture and the legacy of the conflict (see Hayward et al, 2020; Haughy, 2020), but even this document remembered to include the usual platitudes around 'structured and flexible engagement with civic society', and it reinforced the idea that the sector had a role to play in co-designing policy programmes, budgets and strategies (NIO, 2020, 20).[4]

Government's invited spaces, its mechanisms for engagement with the wider sectoral bureaucracy, community development agencies and service-delivery organisations, facilitate discussion of policies that could impact on communities or service users, as well as discussion of issues which impact on and shape the overall relationship between the VCS and government departments. Interviewees suggest that forums, and ongoing engagement and debate, help to bring coherence and an agreed approach to managing the relationship between government and the VCS. As one government official explains in relation to one particular invited space:

'This forum is a mechanism for engagement, and for talking and for listening ... I mean, it gives an opportunity for people to meet and discuss ... both government and the sector felt that there was a mechanism required to make sure that engagement took place regularly.' (Government official)

Extending opportunities for engagement should bring coherence to the way different government departments and VSC agencies deal with each other, and officials stress that cross-sector relationships should not be premised on hierarchical relations that involve one actor in the network (government) doing things to another (the VCS). Through the agreed values and principles of the concordat, the 'rules of play' will be those of mutual respect, partnership and establishing a dialogue between equals.

'What we want to do is make sure that the sector and government are comfortable with those [engagement] processes so that you don't end up with the government doing things to the sector, it's more doing things with the sector ... what the concordat does is set out a set of general rules that sort of says, "right, in any relationship with the voluntary and community sector here is the rules ... here is the way you should treat them and here is the way they should treat you" ... consistency will bring a transparency and accountability ... longer term that should mean we get more efficient and effective governance and a better civil society.' (Government official)

In spaces for engagement that bring together diverse actors from across the VCS and government, there is to be a search for consensus, with issues under discussion agreed 'as a forum'. Indeed, as one official explains, everybody around the table will 'have to agree'. The equitable, consistent and trusting relationships that officials wish to see established between the sector and the departments seem to require some form of bureaucratic ordering and top-down command, but with mechanisms in place for 'talking and for listening', everyone who wishes to be involved will have a seat at the table as part of a process of transparent and accountable engagement.

'There will be no opt-outs. The department of education can't say to the groups they work with, "no we don't want to use that". We will be able to say hold on a minute, your minister signed this, you have to do it. The same with everybody, so they all have to be around the table, and they all have to have their say and they all have to agree to action it … we wanted a transparent and accountable process where the people could say it was inclusive.' (Government official)

Reflecting successive devolved administrations' commitment to openness and government–VCS interaction, politicians are also keen to point out that their door is always open to the CDOs that make up the 'local family of communities'. Again, as in many of the interviews, and in much of the policy and sectoral literature, politicians seem to value their relationship with the VCS because it builds the capacity of the community to do what needs to be done, particularly in terms of normalising NI society and breaking down old barriers.

'Whoever, unionist or nationalist, is coming through the door to say "we have a problem with this funding application or that one", I don't think about that … I think about whether they are part of the local family of communities, if you like, and if they are using their role as community development leaders to promote greater integration and greater normalisation. It is the job of community groups to support communities in their own development, to do the stuff that the state doesn't and shouldn't do, and to bring people together.' (Politician)

In this 'motherhood and apple pie' narrative of a 'family of communities', we can see the influence of ideas that have permeated the policy literature in NI for decades, such as community self-help and communities identifying and taking charge of tackling their own problems. Community groups must also be seen to be 'doing the right thing', suggesting that there are acceptable and unacceptable rules of behaviour. The sector should focus on the needs of the community within which it is embedded, but in line with current fashions within government policy discourses, the sector's work must not take the form of isolated projects, but rather, fit within a joined-up strategy. Projects should be linked in some way and have some strategic direction. The purpose of community development and the sector should be bringing people together in ways that will help with integration, reconciliation, and again, cohesion.

'It needs to go beyond just separate, isolated, independent interventions to solve a specific problem. They need to fit into a much wider strategy. That strategy needs to be built on sound principles of community cohesion ... sound principles of community development ... and in our unique context here they need to be integrated into the objective of building reconciliation.' (Politician)

If there has always been a grassroots networking ethos, then government has certainly tried to capitalise on this by providing spaces for interactions that are both horizontal and vertical in nature. Community development workers suggest that the localised spaces and initiatives that enable vertical and horizontal networking and partnership have allowed sectoral organisations to more effectively locate where responsibilities lie, and they act as useful accountability mechanisms.

'There are a number of networks and partnerships ... there are those partnerships within the city. You can list a number of facilities in terms of both physical space and networks and organisations within the city ... there was a lot of community fora grew up in Belfast, and they were excellent in the sense that they often brought government departments to book about what wasn't being done, and what should be done, and what was done and who was responsible for that. And that's fantastic.' (VCS)

In the language of long-standing governmental narratives, these kinds of forums and networks should contribute to an increase in the structural aspect of both bridging and linking social capital, for there will be an increase in the number of connections as people from different communities and agencies are brought together to focus on particular issues and problems. Evidence of inter-organisational contact that extends beyond the immediate community and that spans gradients of power also provides us with at least a partial picture of an area's civic vibrancy and the openness of the local political opportunity structure. For social capitalists, these types of face-to-face networks constitute social capital because they are regulated by a person's reputation for cooperative endeavour, and individual participants will build trust through recurring interaction (Putnam, 2000, 228–90). Past successes will 'grease the wheels' of further interaction and the network will allow for flows of helpful information that will facilitate the achievement of even larger goals. These kinds of recurring interactions, and the maintenance of networks that facilitate the flow of information, certainly seem to be characteristics of localised networks that bring together community-based organisations with decision makers. As one CDW explains:

'Twenty years ago … if you got politicians around the table to talk about this organisation they would have torn us apart … they didn't understand who we were, what we were. At a meeting one kept banging the table going "where do you get your mandate from, how dare you have an opinion". Politicians are now more interested in coming and talking about how we might work together, you know, it's "are you aware that the council are doing this, and would you be interested in working on it?" So, politicians are much less negative, I think, about the community sector, because we have learned to work together a little bit.' (VCS)

While formalised relationships between community-based organisations and state agencies have a long history in NI, relationships between the sector and politicians had been strained by the fact that local political parties were neutered by direct rule, and over the decades, they became 'jealous and frustrated by the success of the sector' (McCall and Williamson, 2001, 364) and its perceived usurpation of 'the proper functions of elected representatives' (McCall and O'Dowd, 2008, 33; see also Acheson and Milofsky, 2008). In multi-actor partnerships established after the ceasefires there were difficult initial stages of tension and distrust between the VCS and local government actors, 'with councillors claiming they had greater democratic legitimacy and therefore warranted a more prominent position on the partnerships than the voluntary and community members' (Greer, 2001, 759). According to some interviewees working in community-based organisations, informal relationships between the sector and politicians have become more congenial and politicians are less likely to question the legitimacy of locally based organisations. Individual politicians have become more open to the idea of engaging with diverse partners drawn from civil society, and politicians are more likely to encourage community-based actors to take part in government projects and forums. It seems that through interaction, the politicians and sector come to see each other more as partners who can indeed learn 'to work together a little bit'. Through a constant affirmation of the sector's value over the last few decades, and because of the sector acting on its 'moral imperative' to build relationships and networks, the sector has accumulated a mass of formal and informal vertical links. Sectoral organisations are often asked to participate in the formal invited spaces of government consultation and engagement, and the sector (or at least some parts of it) is certainly better connected to the decision-making bureaucracy than the average citizen.

'The sector gets involved in different consultation processes …
in this sector we have access to politicians, if you work for any
of the bigger voluntary organisations, generally you have the
ear of the minister and SPADs[5] or very senior politicians … you
could be out working and you would bump into the minister
or a SPAD.' (VCS)

Those operating in working-class areas also explain that there are spaces
for sector, community and government interaction that are designed
around thematic areas and issues:

'There are government consultation processes, including
consultation with the community, and community and residents'
groups would sit on housing and health forums.' (VCS)

Like many of the forums and vertical interactions mentioned by the
interviewees, invited spaces may be instigated and maintained through
institutional edict, but they are perfect examples of how public bodies
and departments try to realise their promise that they will bring together
a diverse range of voices and feed their expertise into the policymaking
process. For many interviewees, such invited spaces and networks,
when they bring together VCS organisations, activists and decision
makers, have the potential to be 'a force' in those policy areas that are
of concern to VCS organisations. A CDW from a working-class area
was involved in an invited space that was tasked with looking at issues
around poverty and inequality:

'A network established in the house [Stormont], it had political
representation in it, and it had people from a whole range of
active sectors in it that are addressing poverty and disadvantage.
It had every potential to become a force in policy.' (VCS)

In the interviews and government and sectoral literature regarding
partnership, networking and vertical relationship building, there seems
to be a number of assumptions working in the background on the part
of both government and the VCS. Linkages are seen to have value
in and of themselves, separate from any outcome they may produce.
Secondly, grassroots activists, who work in some of the poorest of
communities, see potential in invited spaces. There is a hope that,
if they can have the 'ear' of decision makers, as many interviewees
suggested they do, they can have some influence on policy and
spending decisions.

Networked insiders as agents of change

As voluntary organisations represent diverse communities of interest, it is claimed that they enable a pluralism of expression and that this makes them, to a greater or lesser extent, political organisations (see Milbourne, 2013, 179). As we have seen, the region's VCS organisations are recognised in the corridors of power as advocates for a diverse range of groups, interests and communities, and as they tend to describe themselves as drivers of social and policy change, VCS organisations in NI could also be seen as 'small-p political'. VCS interviewees point to their campaigning and advocacy work as one of the distinguishing characteristics of the sector, and this role is intimately tied up with the idea of the VCS acting as an independent and critical voice in policy discussions. As one interviewee from a regional charity explains:

'Our independence is something we treasure ... our ability to comment on and shift and change policy, that is a prime function of a charitable body ... to address change and address policy, to achieve better outcomes for those whose lives we want to enhance as a function of our charitable purposes.' (VCS)

Ideas about advocacy, of giving voice to and supporting those not represented within traditional democratic structures, are certainly clear themes emerging from the interviews. Interviewees suggest that the VCS provides a critical voice in the decision-making process, and that it uses its formal and informal vertical relationships in its efforts to impact on the thinking of decision makers. Interviewees explained how they have access to ministers, officials, advisors and departmental committees, access which they can use to lobby for policy changes and to influence the decision-making process:

'When it comes to lobbying of politicians, the [voluntary and community] sector is very active, and very critical of political decisions.' (VCS)

'There are lots of parts of the [voluntary and community] sector that are very active in lobbying ... quite strong in terms of policy development and their engagement with politicians ... most of the departmental committees will generally hear from voluntary and community organisations on the topics and issues that concern them ... there are a lot of organisations that are involved in consultations and trying to influence. The great bulk of that [effort to influence decisions] goes on, I wouldn't say under the radar, but there is not a lot of publicity attached to it.' (VCS)

Interviewees suggest that, with its representation of diverse interests, the VCS can drive progressive changes in social and political attitudes, it can inform policy debates, and particularly if it has access to independent sources of revenue through 'enterprising' fundraising activities, it can change policy and practice by example.

> 'There is a big argument to make that the realm of the voluntary and community sector and social movements is where big social change actually takes place, and when public opinion changes in those areas, governments then follow and they make the changes.' (VCS)

> 'By doing things fundamentally differently … we use our services to shift policy … when the conversation changes [around social issues] we are already in the space to demonstrate other ways … our programmes have become mainstream programmes … we have an independence of voice and an independence of action and an independence of revenue so we can do that as a partner as opposed to a tool of government.' (VCS)

Contra the notion that the VCS needs a huge flow of resources, or that it needs to be adversarial to effect change, some interviewees suggest that the mechanism for change is the development of a disposition that values linkages and being connected, participating in the spaces where decisions will ultimately be made and leading by example through innovative practice. Once an organisation develops and values this 'connectionist' disposition (see Davies, 2011a), and once networks have been built, these bridges and links are a resource that can be drawn on strategically. Effectiveness as an organisation (or a community) comes about through finding inroads into the decision-making systems, as well as finding and engaging with new partners. In other words, organisations need to become 'operators'.

> 'You don't need to have lots of resources; you don't need to have money … what voluntary and community groups should be thinking about is how they get more out of other organisations … some very effective people, they engage in everything, and take part, and in terms of representation, get them [the community

or group] involved in everything ... if you are a shrewd operator you can punch way above your weight.' (VCS)

We have already seen that when sector organisations do develop the networking disposition, it gives them privileged access to decision makers (in comparison to other citizens), and many sector organisations seem to have the ability to move confidently inside the governance system. For those working in the policy-development arena, gaining access is 'what works' in terms of the sector having an influence and putting forward an agenda for change. As some officials acknowledge, the sector has come to be seen as the legitimate voice of a diverse range of groups, and this attitude is evidenced by the fact that the sector has been invited into decision-making (or at least, consultation) processes by both politicians and officials.

> 'We are more proactive and meet with people and meet with officials and give presentations ... from my experience that is what works ... you should be doing evidence to the committee all the time ... seeking meetings with the chairs of the committees, really engaging with the Stormont structures.' (VCS)

The sector is aiming to influence other institutions and decisions around the distribution of resources, and therefore the sector must use its insider status and networks to engage with NI's 'messy' system of governance. Perhaps reflecting the commonly held view that NI is over-governed (for a discussion see Birrell, 2012a; Birrell, 2012b), VCS workers stress the importance of insider tactics when the sector is trying to make its voice heard among a multitude of voices emanating from competing sectors and agencies.

> 'In a small place like Northern Ireland, with so many layers of governance, one of the objectives must be to effect policy change, given that some of the community and voluntary organisations are dealing with some of the bigger problems, whether it be health, education, environmental issues. You want to get in there and have an influence, because rest assured, the private sector and the other sectors are having their influential role in where resources are spent.' (VCS)

When decisions over the distribution of resources lead to cuts in areas of work that are undertaken by VCS organisations, the sector pushes back by introducing into the discussion modes of thinking and viewpoints that may be unrepresented in bureaucratic decision-making processes. It can challenge what the VCS perceives as a governmental tendency to see the sector's work as peripheral, and it can challenge any departmental inclination to protect core functions over potentially more valuable activities within the VCS. As an interviewee from a larger charity explains:

'Where [engagement and lobbying] really comes to the fore is when there are clashes over available resources ... government, across all departments, have cut things back very, very sharply ... in squeezed financial circumstances public sector budget holders tend to protect the centre ... they will cut things that they see as peripheral and easy, things that voluntary sector organisations did ... [in implementing some of the cuts] they didn't really consider the worth or value of any of those things ... but they might be more valuable than some of the things that they [government] were carrying on themselves.' (VCS)

Engaging with and lobbying committees, civil servants and ministers, and participating in government's forums and invited spaces, interviewees explain, not only allows the sector to engage in current policy debates. This activity also helps develop some institutional memory within the structures of governance, as decision makers and decision implementers will take the information they glean from the VCS with them as they move up and across the structures of government. In terms of trying to gain access to decision makers and government agencies, the sector is pushing at an open door. Government has repeatedly committed itself to maximising participation in the policymaking process, and both the sectoral and governmental interviewees seem to share the goal of developing relationships that will strengthen the role of the sector and allow it to be an effective partner in both service delivery and policy development.

'We [government departments] have a whole series of actions that we hope will help the relationship [between the VCS and government] ... we are looking at processes that should help voluntary and community organisations operate more effectively and efficiently ... get the money they need rather than get the money that government decides they are going to get ... and maximising participation in procurement, looking at best practice guides, policy development, involvement in policy, so these are all things that we are doing.' (Government official)

With the existence of a well-funded VCS infrastructure and the existence of 'shared' sectoral spaces, the sector can also invite politicians into its own spaces. Through bespoke events and regular forums and policy groups, the sector infrastructure really does seem to reinforce networks and build social capital in the way government hoped it would. The various infrastructure agencies and networks provide physical spaces whereby the sector can share information, and they facilitate the kinds of networking that allows the sector 'to do what needs to be done'. As one interviewee with a role in policy development explains:

> 'The information I got there [at events hosted within infrastructure spaces] I used up at Stormont, you know, so it's really important to my work. They're facilitating events … that is absolutely perfect; they give me the space to do what I need to do.' (VCS)

Access is clearly at the heart of the VCS's ideas and strategies concerning the influencing of decisions, and in the talk of the interviewees from the sector, 'effecting change' is generally thought of as influencing policy and policy implementation, representing diverse interests in policy debates or trying to open up opportunities whereby they can share their expertise and knowledge. Many interviewees express their role as agents of change in terms of the VCS's commitment to social justice and 'progressive' social change, and the interviewees explain how they have, or aim to have, an influence on the discourses that will inform policy decisions across a range of areas. In line with the 'networking ethos' that was evident earlier, organisations use their sectoral horizontal relationships to build coalitions within the sector across thematic areas and traditional social cleavages. These coalitions can bring together local knowledge and expertise and assist in the collection of information and stories that can be used to help frame policy debates or assist in the lobbying of government. This idea of bringing diverse groups into collective endeavours, especially around issues that cut across geographical, social, political and religious barriers, is often central to the way the VCS thinks about its work. Government and the VCS, in the interviews and in policy literature, are always keen to stress that they want to bring into the decision-making process the voice of those who will be most affected by any policy decisions. Welfare reforms implemented by the Coalition government seem to have been a case in point, with the VCS using its position as the voice of diverse interests and communities to put forward to government what the impact of the reforms would be on different groups in the population. With a top-down recognition of the sector's value and 'voice', claims to mutual respect between government and the VCS, and the ability of a well-resourced VCS to invite decision makers into spaces that are created and defined by the sector, it seems that the VCS has the capacity to broaden the conversation about a particular issue. In line with government's claim that continual engagement is required across sectors, and that this engagement brings a diversity of voices into the decision-making process, sectoral interviewees suggest that bringing together diverse actors from across the sector and beyond to discuss pertinent issues broadens the 'critical space' in NI.

'The outcome of a day's [sectoral] conference isn't going to be transformative. But it provides a space where you can hear anyone talk about the issues of inequality, welfare or tax in the same breath. That might change the background music and it's that critical space that needs to be broadened.' (VCS)

The VCS is now embedded within a system whereby a diverse range of partners are involved in creating a complex web of networks, and the aim of these networks is to find solutions to complex issues. Government and the VCS are both committed to developing 'effective partnerships', and both are committed to exploring change and innovation in the nature of government–VCS relationships, in policy development and service delivery, and in the measurement of outcomes (Birrell and Gormley-Heenan, 2015, 203).

VCS pragmatism and innovation

The ideas expressed in the previous section are also related to other common themes in the interviews with VCS representatives, most notably, the notion of sectoral pragmatism, creativity and innovation. That the VCS is a site of creativity, risk taking, innovation and flexibility is a common theme running through the interviews with both community-based and service-delivery organisations. Sector interviewees often suggest that they can work in ways that conflict with the 'acceptable' way of doing things, and when these risks pay-off, the knowledge that has been garnered can be fed into mainstream service delivery and programmes.

'The idea of the [voluntary and community] sector must be that they pilot programmes, run programmes, and if those programmes work they can then be mainstreamed ... the idea of the voluntary and community sector is to help their end users or their clients, but also to be innovative and meet needs. The sector does that, it goes out on a limb, then if it works, gets it mainstreamed. Then it can help others, and other communities and other areas.' (VCS)

In contrast to the purportedly bureaucratically ordered and inflexible services that are delivered by government agencies, the sector's innovative mindset seems to be its unique selling point, particularly in a context where the sector may be trying to engage with individuals who are already, as one interviewee describes it, 'over social-worked'. As those closest to complex problems within a community or service-user group, it is argued that the sector has a unique ability to deliver change because it can identify and respond to needs as and when they arise. The idea of innovation suggests that the sector has the disposition, flexibility and autonomy to change its working practices to suit local conditions and exigencies. Because of its innovative disposition, it is argued, the sector is constantly looking to form new alliances and new and effective partnerships that will 'get things done' at the community level. The sector, in other words, is the embodiment of government's call for creative and innovative approaches to social problems, and it has the capacity to create and seize opportunities.

'Organisations need to be, you know, they need to see that innovation might be their strength. Being innovators, making sure they are striving for new ways of doing things, better ways of meeting needs or looking out for the unmet needs within communities and so on ... if you look historically here, the [VCS] innovations of the past are the mainstream of the future.' (VCS)

The innovative and pragmatic disposition of the VCS helps ensure organisational survival and relevance, but it also allows VCS groups to meet emerging needs, seize opportunities and mould programmes from the inside. As VCS interviewees explain, programmes shift and change as the diverse partners react to unforeseen events or weaknesses in the original design, and these changes are driven by the sectoral workers' on-the-ground knowledge of the problem and what needs to be done to address it. When delivering a service or programme and planning for the future, VCS organisations are also free of the bureaucratic constraints that are placed on a public body.

'Do you stand silent and take the money, or do you shape it into what you need to do? It's a partnership here. Okay, it might be about government deciding what needs to be done, but you have that debate … you say [to government] "you got to look at this, it's not about you coming in here and forcibly implementing anything, because that doesn't work" … it's about understanding that when things are going wrong, you stop, you look around, you look at it again. You know where you need to get to, but it's just getting there.' (VCS)

'You need to be flexible in your plans, and I think that is probably the strength of the voluntary sector in that you are more flexible and you can change direction, you know, we aren't the civil service, we don't have a huge bureaucracy behind us or in front of us, so you can move quickly if something seems like an opportunity.' (VCS)

As noted earlier in the chapter, interviewees from some larger organisations support the idea that, in the name of sectoral diversity, smaller organisations should be able to compete for funding and contracts, and they recognise the need for grant funding of smaller organisations. However, for some interviewees, the shift away from the grant-aid model in recent years has bolstered organisational independence and the potential for creative and 'cross-cutting' work that will deliver change for end users. Government contracts, and the surpluses that can sometimes be derived from them, have allowed organisations to take on new areas of work, diversify their funding base and develop new and innovative approaches to delivering services.

'[By competing for contracts] we don't have a single funding body or commissioning body, and that diversification allows us to work in a variety of policy areas that are important to us … and not be controlled or coordinated.' (VCS)

Though an organisational focus on the idea of surpluses might suggest isomorphism in the direction of the private sector, any unrestricted charitable income can potentially be used by service-providing organisations 'to meet the needs of those overlooked or rejected by the state' (Chater, 2008, 31). Contract surpluses can be used with more discretion by an organisation, it can work in areas that government and other funders aren't necessarily willing to pay for directly, and in doing so, the organisation won't have to follow the prescriptive criteria that is often attached to other funding. Some interviewees also suggest that competition and access to surpluses helps push up performance and innovative practice within the sector, and that it spurs on intra-sectoral partnership working while weeding out organisations that aren't performing.

Conclusion

This chapter has illustrated how important the notions of partnership working, networks and 'being connected' have become in the way VCS workers, politicians and officials think about and understand the role of the sector within Northern Irish society and its institutional landscape. It has illustrated how government and the sector draw on the language of networks, connectedness and relationship building to explain what they do and what they achieve when they are trying to deal with complex problems. For individuals working in the sector, at all levels and across a range of thematic areas, there is a belief that the sector has an unmatched ability to bring local expertise and knowledge to networked decision-making processes, and that this ability is a key component of the VCS's value. We have seen how narratives promote the idea that the sector is a wealth of knowledge, a site of innovative practice and a voice for marginalised communities and service-user groups. As Birrell and Gormley-Heenan (2015, 184) suggest, 'the establishment of devolution gave rise to anticipated tension between the community sector and elected representatives, but in practice the Executive acknowledged the advantage of a vibrant and extensive voluntary and community sector'. Certainly, there is little in the literature or the interview data that would suggest that politicians in NI would continue to publicly subscribe to the view that 'it is time for the sector to stand aside' (member of the Legislative Assembly quoted in McCall and Williamson, 2001, 365), or that politicians believed that they needed to 'claw back the power and influence lost to the sector' (see McCall and Williamson, 2001, 365).

As the interviewees suggest, politicians, as well as the departments, actively seek out the help and knowledge of the VCS. A clear theme emerging from the interviews is that one of the roles of the VCS is linking disadvantaged communities with those who hold power and resources, and government actions would suggest that it has recognised the VCS as the legitimate voice of different groups and communities. Networks, funding relationships and forums for discussion allow policymakers to draw in the localised and specialised knowledge of an ever-expanding range of new partners and collaborators from the VCS. Decades of network boosterism would appear to have led to fundamental changes in the political opportunity structure at the local and regional level, with VCS organisations building up a wealth of political and departmental contacts, both formal and informal. In the institutional landscape of post-conflict NI, the language of networks, access, linkage, relationships and social capital would appear to describe a shift to what could be characterised as networked, post-traditional or non-hierarchical ways of tackling difficult issues.

From these interviews, we can also see that government policy and rhetoric has helped frame the way the VCS describes itself, drawing on ideas such as partnership, collaboration, innovation, involvement, participation, community self-help and community confidence. These ideas have been central to the narrative of third-way policymakers across the UK (Imrie and Raco, 2003, 47; Kearns, 2003, 39) and Europe (Kendall, 2009; Enjolras et al, 2018). Discourses about the role and nature of the VCS and its vertical relationships seem to be shared and co-constructed by government, grassroots organisations, service-delivery organisations, funders and infrastructure organisations. The VCS has come to be seen as an essential player in the search for and implementation of policies that will help to address the region's difficult problems, and in particular, its community relations problems.

Horizontally, the networks that develop out of inter-organisational relationship building at the local level appear to promote a sense of trust, building and sustaining social capital and adding to economic and social development. It is claimed that these relationship-building practices are addressing post-conflict issues by creating informal and state-backed bridges between fragmented communities, with the VCS acting as a vanguard in the development of risk-taking and innovative approaches in community relations, advocacy and service delivery. Intra-sector and cross-sector relationships are described in terms that suggest that they are social capital in action, with partnerships allowing diverse actors to work together in coalition, and consultative forums and networks allowing thematic groups and communities to articulate their needs and issues. The talk of the interviewees would suggest that the concordat's 'shared vision' of government and the VCS working 'together as social partners' is well on its way to becoming a reality (DSD, 2011, 2). However, as the next two chapters will illustrate, this chapter has presented just one representation of internal sectoral relationships and the sector's relationships with government, and developments at a political, economic and discursive level are complicating some of the processes and activities described here.

FOUR

Inside the networks: the rhetoric and the reality

Chapter Three presented a particular representation of voluntary and community action, networks, relationship building and civil society–government engagement. The interviewees suggested that networks and connectedness promote the development of social capital and allow different actors to come together to discuss issues, share information and deal with problems impacting on communities or specific groups. One of the claims made for having the 'special relationship' between the VCS and government is that the VCS acts as 'advocates for communities, families and people', and that it provides a unique insight into community need (DSD, 2011). Officials certainly recognise the funded and service-providing sector as advocates for specific groups, and decades of network and partnership boosterism, together with substantial funding for the development of civil society, certainly seems to have created enough spaces and mechanisms for this 'unique insight' to be put forward to government.

It could be argued that this investment in the VCS has created the connections and infrastructure that allow for a fundamentally new approach to governance, where voices that contradict bureaucratic calculations and dominant opinions are afforded a place in decision-making processes. It would seem that this investment has created a new environment where traditional ways of doing things are not necessarily seen as the best way, and that there is room for the VCS's purported tendency towards innovative practice. This is governance that seemingly links disparate and subordinate and dominant groups in joint ventures, where the participants value new ideas and innovative practices. The interviews paint a picture of a form of governance that harnesses all the talents, skills and knowledge of diverse actors. Rather than dictates and hierarchical relationships being the organising mechanism, the partnerships bring diverse actors together to work in a spirit of cooperativeness. The different interests will jointly identify and define problems and issues, and 'pull in the same direction' in their efforts to address these problems. The VCS, in this story, is more than a mere policy implementer or service-delivery agent. Instead, the interviewees frame the VCS as a lobbyist for social and policy change, and a valued and influential insider to the decision-making process. Its linking social capital – its embeddedness within vertical multi-actor networks – is one of the mechanisms by which it can achieve this influence and change. This networking ethos and ability allows the VCS, service-user groups and communities to 'punch above their weight'.

In the third-way ideal of a networked society, hierarchical interventions and government programmes that send in 'the experts' but ignore community organisations (Blair, 1999, quoted in Halpern, 2005, 284) would no longer be tolerated, and as has already been suggested in previous chapters, in NI the third-way and EU-led rhetoric of investment in civil society and social capital was taken to its extreme. There was, it would seem, a mass of opportunities for 'the community' to engage in the decisions that affect their lives, and large amounts of funding directed to the VCS organisations that could purportedly 'get things done' (Blair, 1999, quoted in Halpern, 2005, 284). Descriptions of the relationship between government and the VCS are smothered in both technocratic and 'motherhood and apple pie' concepts, with both the VCS and government drawing on the language of problem solving, partnership, social capital and 'better governance' to convey what they see as a shared networking and relationship-building ethos. At the rhetorical level, government has explicitly recognised the VCS's claim to a legitimate role in trying to influence governance structures and the decisions that will affect the sector and its users. At the practical level, government has created spaces that allow for government–VCS interaction, and it has tried to facilitate the sector's lobbying role. However, in this chapter we will see that a range of other representations of VCS activity, networks and partnerships are possible, particularly when those embedded within them are drawn into a dialogue about the politics and economics of partnership (Davies, 2011a) and voluntary and community activity.

'Marriages of convenience' and the roll out of market norms

The interviewees made it clear that the motivation for building informal and formal networks, forums and partnerships is that these allow for recurring interaction across existing community, agency and bureaucratic boundaries, and that they allow for face-to-face contact and the development of relationships. A common theme among the responses of VCS interviewees is that their networks provide gateways into 'other' communities, thus giving the wider population the confidence and security to interact across traditional cleavages. The principal driver for this work, according to many of the interviewees, is that VCS organisations have an ethos and a tendency towards pragmatic relationship building. As interviewees noted earlier, relationship building has become something of a 'moral imperative', in that it allows the VCS to come together and engage in cooperative behaviour around common interests. Some interviewees, however, are sceptical of a joint government–VCS narrative that tries to suggest that disparate groups build links because they wish to collaborate to achieve common goals. This sceptical reading of a supposed collaborative ethos is based around the idea that one of the main motivations for horizontal 'collaboration' will be accessing funding, and once that funding is awarded, any meaningful interaction between the groups may be minimal and time-bound. As two CDWs explained:

'Organisations are supposed to collaborate with each other ... there's a long history here of joint applications, and in some cases, they are full partnerships that work well. But a lot of partnerships are, you know, you stick your name down on that there and we'll split the money 50/50 and we'll see you when we report back.' (VCS)

'To be genuinely fair to this sector it builds allegiances and alliances by default. I don't want to be pejorative and say it is funding led, but it is certainly funding inspired.' (VCS)

There is a view among some interviewees that collaboration is pragmatic in that it is driven by a desire to secure funds from funding bodies. If the funding is awarded, the community groups will split the money to deliver projects in their respective communities, but the interaction across community or agency boundaries will be limited and focused merely on meeting some predetermined targets. In some areas, interviewees also explain that while partnerships and networks provide for some limited contact between community activists, this is unlikely to be scaled up to the general population.

'There is some places where there is genuine collaboration happening, but a lot of it is pragmatic, you know, if we work together, we will look to the Community Relations Council and it will draw down a few bob, "you take your few bob and we'll take ours and we will get on with it" ... where I live there is a measure of interaction between activists, but there isn't between the general population.' (VCS)

The establishment of collaborative partnerships that are merely funding-driven 'marriages of convenience' and questions around the extent to which formal partnerships are actually working to achieve a shared vision have been long recognised in the governance literature (see Greer, 2001). The need to secure much-needed resources for the community and a collaborative ethos can exist simultaneously, but the issue of funding-driven partnerships being wrapped up in an optimistic language of relationship building, trust and 'values' and equitable collaboration is a theme that interviewees return to repeatedly. Organisations coming together around shared goals and visions, the desire for independently determined community-level solutions, or a spirit or ethos of cooperation, do not appear to be the driving forces behind the development of networks and partnerships in some geographic and policy areas. Once established, there may only be a modest commitment to genuine partnership practice and collaboration within a network. As the CDW interviewees reflect on the practice of horizontal networking, they can become increasingly sceptical of overblown and overly optimistic accounts of the sector's capacity to independently build, from the bottom up, broad-based relationships that span community divisions. They also seem sceptical of taken-for-granted claims about a collaborative ethos driving VCS practices.

In the experience of some interviewees, the VCS tends to speak about itself in ways that reproduce the story government tells about the sector in any given discursive moment. Government suggested that the VCS was a source of social capital, and hence the sector became, in the story told about itself, a source of social capital. Now government wants to see collaborative effort as the catalyst for efficiency and rationalisation, and so now the VCS has a collaborative ethos. As a number of interviewees point out, the most interesting observation about the role and position of today's VCS is not that it has become a delivery agent of services that follow a 'predetermined script' written by government (Acheson, 2013, 10), but rather that there is a casual lack of concern in some quarters that the sector finds itself in this position. In such circumstances, it is unsurprising that the nomenclature that surrounds the VCS begins to reflect governmental ideologies and priorities.

'Funding here is very much driven by what the funder wants, it's not about the outputs that organisations want to achieve.

The terminology changes all the time … now it's mergers and collaboration. But you have to play that game, by playing that funding game, you have to use the terminology that the departments or that the funders want you to use.' (VCS)

As some interviewees point out, the modest commitment to genuine partnership may be driven by the fact that the 'quality' of the relationships within a given partnership are a 'soft' outcome that wouldn't necessarily be measured or rewarded by funders. Sectoral interviewees have argued that 'it's what gets built at the grassroots, the local infrastructure, the local relationships' that really matters. Yet what gets built at the grassroots has often been engineered through top-down funding mechanisms; the collaboration is often superficial and its sustainability is to a large extent determined by government funding. As opposed to the claim that the sector is imbued with a spirit of cooperation, the mass of networks, partnerships and collaborations can just as easily be explained by the funding-driven need to follow what one interviewee calls the 'next bloody remit'.

As noted in Chapter Two, in connectionist discourses networks come to be rooted in trust as participants build on past achievements, and previous collaborative successes create a template for future collaboration. However, many sectoral interviewees' experiences would seem to invalidate this positive reading of past cooperative efforts. They explain that all the organisations in the geographic or thematic area are in constant competition for the same funds, and despite previous collaborations and relationship building, in this competitive environment relations between the different organisations are to some extent antagonistic.

'You can do all the relationship building that you like, and then there is this pot of money that you need and they need. You know they need it; they know we need it. Off you go, the race starts … we will come together to work on things, but the real relationship underneath can be quite competitive. That's very difficult. Both in terms of a different culture and ethos within organisations, but also, it's really shitty when you have a relationship with an organisation and suddenly you're in competition for the same funds.' (VCS)

The idea of partnership and being connected to other agencies has for decades been a core theme of funding priorities, though the rhetorical fluff that surrounds this agenda seems to change from time to time.

However, as collaboration was often an externally driven instrumental process that was engaged in regardless of any norms or theories of practice, the rhetoric of intra-sectoral collaboration has become incompatible with an increasingly competitive funding framework.

'When we are all being funded, everyone is happy to work with everybody … but as soon as someone says, "shit we are in for a 20 per cent cut of our fund", what are you going to do? … You can't come to a gentleman's agreement … social capital, or whatever you want to call it, can never survive the economics of it.' (VCS)

There are manifest contradictions between the efforts to develop trust-based networks that can facilitate the flow of information, and top-down policies that seek to locate VCS organisations as the bridge between geographical and user-group communities, with a competitive funding framework. In an environment where relationships between organisations are inherently competitive, it would be illogical for organisations to share skills, knowledge and resources, for this sharing could put organisations at a competitive disadvantage.

'When we are in difficult times, when there is a notion of scarcity of resources, it increases competition amongst organisations. The danger of that is that people keep things to themselves, they keep information to themselves, because they are thinking "well if everyone else knows the pot I am bidding into they might bid into it as well, and that might increase the competition".' (VCS)

It seems that, despite the plethora of networks and forums that exist in the region, some relationships and political and bureaucratic connections may be more knowledge rich and valuable than others, for if there was perfect access to information this kind of 'knowledge protectionism' would be impossible. Antagonistic relationships that arise out of competition within the VCS industry, with all organisations competing for their market share of government funding and protecting their operational territory, seem to trump the networking and 'putting-the-community-first' ethos.

'Within this [sub]sector there is huge fragmentation because whoever government funds then there's a row with who they haven't funded. So, you can spend a quarter of your time dealing with those things, instead of doing what you're supposed to be doing ... government funding has made that happen and tendering and competition.' (VCS)

It is important not to exaggerate the uniqueness of today's intra-sectoral and government–VCS relationships. At any given moment, the climate for state–VCS partnership and inter-organisational relationships will be a mishmash of past relations, trends and debates, and these come together to give the impression of a new era (for a discussion see Coule and Bennet, 2018). Even in the post-financial crisis economic environment, policy documents continued to be suffused with connectionist rhetorical artefacts left over from the New Labour boom years. However, many interviewees do believe that competition has intensified, and that the value base of the sector has begun to shift away from collaboration to territorialism. It can sometimes be the case that relations between organisations have become soured in the competitive funding environment, including relations between those organisations that outsiders might assume are aligned around common interests.

'Groups in the sector had to become businesses. You are run as a business, in all the ways, and its territorialism. It's just heartbreaking sometimes, but it is in every single sector. In some sectors they kill each other.' (VCS)

Even 'the weak ties' of the social capital theorists (Granovetter, 1973), the relationships that developed out of previous collaborative efforts and shared interests, can dissolve in a competitive system that promotes opportunism, the withholding of information and inter-organisational antagonism. The competition is guided, from the perspective of many sectoral interviewees, by an ethos that privileges organisational survival. Rather than the cooperative alliances and negotiations around shared interests that the sector was supposed to engender, there is a culture of empire building, conflict and monopolisation.

'The competition is fierce but it is also really, really dirty ... there are people who, at all costs, it's about "we are going to exist and I am going to keep it open", but are you really thinking about who you are working for? I mean, they will do anything, they will trample over the top of you.' (VCS)

'There is a professional cadre of community workers in Northern Ireland ... we have a paradigm of sustainability that means it is about getting more than the other. It is about preserving our organisation. All organisations are just a vehicle for getting things done, it shouldn't be about "the job is to preserve this organisation and it is best placed". How do you know you are going to be best placed to do this work in ten years' time? Things change.' (VCS)

Many of the interviewees agree that this 'keep it open at all costs' mentality – regardless of whether or not the existence of a particular organisation is the best option for meeting the needs of the group or community – is now a defining part of the VCS's psyche. According to interviewees, an ethos of empire building means that success and progress are now measured in financial rather than social or political terms.

'The difficulty you can get sometimes is you can get people judging their success by the amount of money they have raised, as opposed to what's the impact on the community, what's the levels of empowerment and so on … having good community development ethos and values is looking at the needs of the communities and people you are serving and saying "who else do we need to be working with around that", rather than building this empire.' (VCS)

Rather than a cooperative and mutually supportive ethos guiding current practice in the sector, competition within the sector leads to jealousy and resentment about others' successes, and it would seem to be the case that any ethos of collaboration has given way to a new competitive rationality.

'There needs to be recognition made in the sector, particularly by some groups, that you have to leave room for others … there was one point when it looked like breaking point for us and there was a few people standing on the side-lines going "they have bitten off more than they can chew, I can't wait 'till they choke".' (VCS)

It is with this increasingly competitive sector that civil servants are trying to engage. Though there is recognition that people's careers and livelihoods often rely on a particular organisation securing funding and contracts, some officials suggest that in a culture where organisational survival is prioritised it becomes more difficult to engage with the sector in discussions regarding the setting of priorities and the distribution of available resources. As one government official explains, the prioritisation of organisational survival negatively influences processes around 'sensible decision making', while another official suggests that protectionism and competition appear to contradict the notion of a shared collaborative ethos within the sector.

> 'They are all competing with each other, which is against the principles of community development around collaboration that they are supposed to be representing. It's like dog eat dog out there … and you can understand that because it's people's livelihoods, so there is going to be protectionism in there.' (Government official)

The sizeable and generous funding brought about by international responses to the peace process, and NI's embrace of a third-way narrative that celebrates the role of civil society, has helped create a professionalised VCS bureaucracy. Within and between the different thematic sectors of this bureaucracy, actors are in direct conflict with each other as they strive to be included in different resource-transfer networks. There may be a moral imperative for VCS organisations to ask 'who else do we need to be working with', but the desire to sustain the organisation and its share of funding, appear to be more important than putting into practice the partnership ethos the sector claims to have.

Siloed working, organisational change and the trend towards monopolisation

It seems to be the case that even if the claims to a cooperative ethos as laid out in Chapter Three are genuine, this ethos would clash with the realities of a funding system that pits organisation against organisation, identity group against identity group and community against community. Rather than seeing a shared commitment within the sector to working together through networks, some interviewees argue that funding has embedded organisations within a system of thematic silos, with organisations hoping to take ownership of distinct client groups or geographical communities.

> 'It's a very divided sector, just as government is with its silo mentality, the sector has a silo mentality. If you work in the youth sector, you focus on youth issues, if you work in the older persons' sector you are focused on the older persons' issues. You know, we talk about silo mentalities of government, but that can just as well be applied to the voluntary and community sector.' (VCS)

'The funding environment is very siloed, you wouldn't have a neighbourhood strategy that includes everybody ... [service-user groups and strategies] are in silos, rather than thinking that a piece of work should be for everyone ... it's forcing people to change their principles, to take ownership of a group [of service users] and work with that group in order to get the money ... and people are building empires as a result.' (VCS)

As we have already seen, there can exist a culture in the sector whereby organisations are unwilling to share information about the potential 'pots' they are bidding into, lest it 'increase the competition'. There are, therefore, structural and psychological barriers to the development of an ethos whereby sectoral organisations will even begin to think in terms of partnership or co-delivery. Some interviewees work within organisations that, by their very nature, facilitate interactions that span the thematic silos of the sector. For some of these interviewees, many organisations now focus their efforts on building vertical patron–client relationships with the departments that provide their funding. With organisations beginning to replicate the departmental silos of government, organisations no longer aim to build the horizontal relationships that are, according to the rhetoric, necessary to deal with complex problems. Building vertical relationships that will yield funding is now the priority.

'An organisation like ours would be sort of saying, well look, the older people's groups should be talking to younger people's groups in terms of intergenerational work. But actually, if their priority is where are they getting their next funding from, and that next funding is only from the Department of Health and Social Services, well then, that is where they will focus.' (VCS)

Outside of mandated funding-driven partnerships, the sector may be less willing and able to facilitate bridging between social groups with shared interests than some of the 'collaboration and partnership' rhetoric would suggest. Now that surviving the competitive funding environment seems to be the main 'shared goal' of the sector, there is little reason for an organisation to invest in the building of horizontal relationships. Vertical linkages with government and other funders will be more financially fruitful, and horizontal linkages are a potential threat to future funding and ownership of a service-delivery 'space'.

One of the key processes captured by this research is an ongoing 'distancing' (Clayton et al, 2016) between larger and/or regional voluntary bodies and the small and medium-sized organisations. This distancing is driven by a sense that larger organisations are monopolising available resources. As one interviewee explains, after the financial crisis, 'everybody got poorer but the [larger organisations in the] voluntary sector got richer'. This perception that the current environment favours larger organisations would seem to be grounded in reality. NICVA's *State of the Sector* publications show that, over time, larger organisations are capturing a greater proportion of the available resources. Interviewees explain that service contracts have been scaled up in ways that exclude many small and medium-sized organisations, and some smaller organisations have a 'partnership' with a private sector or regional VCS organisation. As Acheson (2014, 10) has suggested, this supply-chain funding model makes organisations accountable to other VCS actors, thereby 'fundamentally changing relations within the sector'. A 'lead partner' model is also used by other funders in the delivery of particular projects, which again leaves partner organisations feeling accountable to another VCS organisation. With the consolidation of contracts and the closure of networks around a few well-placed organisations, some interviewees suggest that rather than a myriad of organisations delivering small projects at a local level, resource-transfer networks will increasingly revolve around large organisations that are wholly dependent on government contracts for services and salaries. For many decades the sector has claimed that it was a sphere for collaborative citizen action that cuts across social divides and thematic silos, and that it was operating from a distinctive value base. However, in a cut-throat funding environment, and despite the repeated claims of 'valuing sectoral diversity', some interviewees working in small or medium-sized organisations believe that larger organisations have little motivation to 'leave room for others'.

> 'One of the people in our network put so much work into getting a project up and running, all his own work, doing it on a shoestring, taking the time to go out and recruit volunteers and users. It was going great, then the department put it out for tender. In swoops [a larger voluntary organisation] and wins the tender. Why is a big organisation applying for such small amounts of money? ... Why are they [small projects] going out for tender? Within months you never heard of the project again because they didn't have the local networks to deliver it.' (VCS)

Across the UK, the VCS has experienced rapid growth and professionalisation as it became increasingly involved in the delivery of public services (Buckingham, 2012). Although successive governments have introduced strategies for the promotion of volunteering, localism and community-level renewal, they have also preferred to work with professionalised organisations. As these large professionalised organisations try to chase bigger contracts and more resources, it is the view of some interviewees that 'well-placed and prominent' organisations have morphed into mini versions of their departmental patrons. As other research suggests, VCS actors have adopted a wide range of practices and organisational cultures that are associated with the private and public sectors (see Rees and Mullins, 2016), often as a result of trying to outdo private-sector and VCS competitors. There is a top-down or coercive element to this isomorphism, with organisations being pushed towards the adoption of a particular form of organisational structure and culture by their funding patrons. As one interviewee seems to suggest, by making imperceptible changes over a long period of time in response to external drivers, an organisation can significantly alter its culture and structure:

'You make wee small changes that don't seem important at the time, then you look back ten years later and the organisation is unrecognisable.' (VCS)

There are top-down and bottom-up drivers of this organisational change, and, as another VCS interviewee seems to suggest, the 'pull' of the rewards that come with winning contracts motivates organisations to mimic the dominant or acceptable practices of other sectors:

'The volunteer organisations are becoming mirror images of the statutory organisations, that's tending to happen, and it's a push/pull factor, you know, they feel like they have to be like that to get the contracts.' (VCS)

Top-down directives and isomorphic pressures therefore nudge organisations onto a trajectory whereby they become mini versions of their departmental patrons or their private sector competitors, and this is in a sector that is already rigid, hierarchical and largely unquestioning of its role in society and its everyday practices.

'Many of the organisations here, they ape the private and the statutory sector, they are hierarchical in their structure and governance, there is an attitude that there is a way of doing things, and that that is the way you ought to do the things, they are conservative with a small c ... there is evidence that community and voluntary organisations aren't as good as they think they are, or as innovative as they think they are. Is there enough critical self-analysis?' (VCS)

In response to the perceived monopolisation of funding by larger organisations, and because of government's rationalisation processes, many organisations fear they are becoming 'bid candy'. The smaller organisations feel that they add to the bids of the corporate service delivery sector or private sector by virtue of their purported connectivity with the community or service-user groups, but that they become the junior partners in any future arrangement. Some interviewees feel that, as government tries to create economies of scale in service provision, larger agencies will try to harvest their knowledge, skills and networks to prove to funders that they can reach a target group. As interviewees pointed out in the previous chapter, community-based organisations see themselves as 'excelling' at meeting the needs of 'hard-to-reach groups' that government can't reach. However, for some interviewees, this inability to reach the most marginalised also applies to large, 'disconnected' voluntary agencies.

'Regional organisations are shooting in and they do the bare minimum ... they don't have the people on the ground, they don't know who the people are, so the first thing they do when they get the contract is ring us ... and I don't think they deliver on the ground.' (VCS)

'There needs to be more differentiation between the big voluntaries that are literally delivering the public services and the community groups that can reach people.' (VCS)

For many interviewees, in the near future, government's resource-transfer networks will be exclusive networks, dominated by well-placed organisations that have the ability and capacity to play the bureaucratic funding game and deliver large-scale services. For interviewees from small and medium-sized organisations in particular, the extent to which prominent organisations have the on-the-ground connections needed to deal with complex problems is a secondary concern for service commissioners, and there is a sense that the well-funded service-providing organisations will be able capture an ever-larger slice of the funding cake due to their superior human, social and financial resources and expertise.

'My concern about the future is that you will have a number of very prominent organisations who will be very good at describing what they do in terms of what the funder wants, whereas you will have grassroots organisations who won't be that sophisticated, or won't have those resources to be able to commit to the writing up of tenders or applications. A lot of the money will go to organisations who talk the talk but can't deliver, or don't have the networks to deliver.' (VCS)

This observation that an ability to 'talk the talk' may have become just as important as a record of delivery on the ground reflects longstanding processes. Since the capacity-building and partnership rhetoric reached its zenith in the wake of the GFA, dominant notions of community and organisational 'capacity' have often 'prioritised professionally completed funding applications rather than the effective delivery of inclusive community development' (Kilmurray, 2017, 249). For many interviewees, the scaling up of contracts, and the imposition of a tendering and procurement process that is difficult for some organisations to navigate, has been driven by government's need to demonstrate efficiency savings within more tightly constrained budgets. However, these processes of 'scaling up' and consolidation are also seen as being driven by a governmental aspiration to simplify its relationship with the sector. It is certainly the case that in some policy areas, UK and NI administrations have changed procurement practices, and recalibrated 'the provider market to reduce transaction costs associated with managing multiple contracts' (Wiggan, 2015, 119). As resources and contracts become increasingly concentrated within a few prominent organisations that are able to survive and compete in such an environment, some of the interviewees argue that there is a need to redefine what the VCS is, and who is included in any definition of it.

'It would be a good piece of work to go back to the creation of one of these big organisations and find its original mission statement and see how that came out as this massive organisation. They are organisations employing hundreds of people. I can't see where the voluntary and community aspect is. They are businesses run by voluntary organisations.' (VCS)

'There's people in the sector that shouldn't be here at all ... if you are doing something that is meeting government targets ... if you are a service provider, you are providing services for government, I don't call you a community organisation, I'm not even sure, completely personally, I would say you are a voluntary organisation. You are a service provider and you are a business, which is operating like a social-economy business, more or less.' (VCS)

For some interviewees, there is nothing particularly novel about the way in which funding streams can be monopolised by a few large agencies as, historically, funding has tended to be rationalised and regionalised over time. As noted earlier in the chapter, the existing climate for government–VCS partnerships and inter-organisational relationships is often a mixture of past relations, trends and debates which come together to give the impression of a new era (Coule and Bennet, 2018). For some interviewees, today's concerns and debates about diversity in the area of service delivery, and the reworking and rescaling of funding streams, are similar to previous rationalisations of major funding sources.

'What we're likely to see happening is what we saw happen in the 1980s with the ACE scheme. ACE started off as being very diffuse … but then gradually over a decade it would be brought down to about 20 large providers who would have done West Belfast or something like that. I think the same thing will happen with tenders, and indeed we've already seen it … so, you know, it's limited that you would get a tender just for a small geographical area because they will be for a health board area or a Northern Ireland-wide area.' (VCS)

This seems to be a prescient observation, for over the last number of years the local networks of community organisations have seen jobs lost, and the closure of projects and organisations, as government has regionalised projects and the delivery of services.

'We have watched many projects, many of whom were really good, close in the last 18 months as the department has tapered its funding and is going for the more regional focus rather than localised. And, you know, those activists are out of work, who have maybe 20 or more years' experience, who can't find funding anywhere, and it's an awful waste.' (VCS)

Some community organisations do have enough capacity to compete for and win relatively large pieces of work, but even here we see regrets concerning how top-down funding mechanisms, and the sector's bottom-up response to the funding environment, has shifted the focus of community-based organisations away from the local issues they were set up to address.

> 'Some of the things they talk about, being overarching and working across the community, is putting a lot of strain on the community groups ... you are working across a number of communities and you are working city-wide, and that takes away from a lot of your locally based work.' (VCS)

These comments also suggest that, among some interviewees, there is little meaningful buy-in to the technocratic and managerialist discourses that surround the scaling up of services and regionalisation. In this view, the 'loss of local focus' has been hidden behind a rhetoric that celebrates being 'overarching' and 'working across the community'. This brings us back to the previous interviewee's warning that resource-transfer networks will eventually close around 'prominent organisations who are good at describing what they do in terms of what the funder wants', for it seems natural that those most competent in the use of this technocratic language should succeed. Rather than creating the conditions for a dynamic system of networks, the closure of resource-transfer networks around those who are confident in speaking the language of the latest managerial 'fad' will produce a sector that is both more streamlined and a more 'governable terrain' (Carmel and Harlock, 2008, 155). Organisations can be included or excluded according to their capacity to describe their work in the technocratic language of 'sound procurement' and efficient and quantifiable performance.

> 'They, the funders, have all bought into this outcome-based accountability, they can't talk about anything else, impact and outcomes is all they talk about ... I have experienced a lot of these things in different guises and under different titles. You have to almost learn a new language to talk to these people, and to make them understand that your work is valuable.' (VCS)

Resource dependency, organisational survival and adapting to a changing environment

There is a natural tendency within some VCS organisations to view their particular field of work as a priority, and in the view of some sectoral and government interviewees, this privileging of the work of one's own organisation has clouded thinking around priority setting and sensible decision making about the distribution of resources. Rather than discussions around the allocation of funding being grounded in objective, needs-based assessments, both government and sectoral interviewees suggest that these discussions are often guided by the prioritisation of organisational survival. Some government interviewees are firm in their view that there has been a 'shift to funding what is needed as opposed to what is available', and some government interviewees suggest that there needs to be more recognition from the sector that self-interest may be setting the tone of their discussions with government funders.

> 'There are conflicts here which the sector probably needs to be a little bit more disciplined in managing, you are speaking to them as advocates for the people they are representing, but at the same time they can be the providers of a service and therefore there is a degree of self-interest, organisational interest, in the discussions that is not always fully transparent.' (Government official)

The shift to funding 'what is needed rather than what is available', and a more open recognition of the VCS's dependency and self-interested motivations, represents a cultural and discursive change. In previous eras, when decision makers needed some mechanism for contact with the governed, they seemed to have taken the view that VCS organisations had value in and of themselves, and they wanted to build and support a diverse ecosystem of civil-society organisations. Government's more instrumentalist approach towards the sector, and its hierarchical agenda setting, is often clashing with decades of rhetoric, exigencies and structures that had secured the role of the sector in network governance and partnership arrangements. These discourses had suggested that statutory–civil society networks could help address complex social problems by allowing diverse agencies to come together to both define problems and design and deliver solutions. However, this entrenched rhetoric of partnership, diversity and collaboration doesn't align with new models of top-down procurement that promote monopolisation, and that seek to make service delivery networks more simplified and governable. Today's models for VCS funding are founded on very different principles in comparison to past eras, and the thinking among some decision makers in NI seems to have shifted so that it unapologetically reflects the more instrumentalist, transactional and efficiencies-driven approach to the VCS that we see in wider UK government policy narratives.

'Procurement, at its very basis, has the idea that you know exactly what you want to procure, you know what you want to buy, and you maybe put it out to the lowest bidder … it has no interest in the type of organisation … [in some service areas] if we just see it as a transaction, that anyone could deliver these services, that we will tender and contract for it, as the trend now is, eventually you will lose all the [VCS] organisations.' (VCS)

'The departments' thinking is always top-down … they came with a fait accompli, it's not a co-design … a co-design is something that everyone should be striving for, so there is no point in them coming with it already written.' (VCS)

Procurement, and the transition away from grant support for a diverse sector, are a clear move away from the civil society boosterism of the peace process era, and recent consultations and 'toolkits' suggest a subtle shift in tone in government's rhetoric concerning the relationship between government and the VCS. In the past, government had argued that the sector was well placed to help build better relationships within and between communities, it was lauded as the 'glue holding society together' and it enjoyed a celebratory rhetoric concerning its purported contribution to democracy and peacebuilding. The vague communitarianism of the New Labour era appears to be an ineradicable 'go to' language for beginning any discussion of the VCS in NI. Therefore, the more recent policy documentation still contains rhetorical artefacts from the 'golden age' of government–VCS relations, with government claiming that it wants to support and harness the energy and social capital which exists in communities (DfC, 2017). However, representing a significant shift in emphasis since the New Labour and post-GFA heyday, and in language that is strikingly similar to that employed by Conservative government ministers, this policy documentation argues that the VCS should become more sustainable, transition away from reliance on grant-based funding where possible, and move towards a structure in which income is linked to the delivery of services and outcomes (DfC, 2016; DfC, 2017). NI's government departments are now seeking to help third sector organisations develop the skills and knowledge they will need to 'raise investment', access a more diverse range of income sources and survive the 'significant challenges in relation to a much tighter public funding environment' (DfC, 2016, 4). For a number of interviewees, the 'fashion' for procurement in government circles and the transition away from a reliance on grant-based funding, seems to represent a shift to top-down models whereby commissioners determine needs, problems and solutions, and then procure services accordingly. However, many sectoral interviewees take the view that this competitive and top-down model disadvantages those smaller organisations that bring added value through their longstanding connection to service users and communities.

'Your notion was that anyone could deliver this service, but if they [service deliverers] are not in tune with their community, people won't go there anymore ... there will be a point in time when people will say "there used to be a whole load of organisations that did useful things. Where are they now?" ... the procurement process will destroy that [diversity].' (VCS)

From at least the mid-1990s and through the 2000s, the region was being bombarded by unprecedented levels of rhetoric that celebrated the role of civil-society organisations, and this rhetoric was coupled with generous levels of funding for the VCS. These discourses were built on an assumption that there was value in the existence of a VCS organisation, irrespective of any objective or measurable contribution to society. The level of resources that flowed to the voluntary and community industry, and the number of forums, partnerships and networks that were created, helped sustain the rhetoric of a healthy, vibrant, diverse, connected and consulted sector. Even in relatively small geographic areas, a number of organisations could be the beneficiaries of funding from one source or another (Shirlow and Murtagh, 2004, 62). A history of dependency on top-down funding, and decades of socialisation into a funding 'normality' which was in fact exceptional, has meant that the period of rationalisation, regionalisation and the winding down of the activities of international funders was often met with despondency (see also Knox and Quirk, 2016, 241). Some organisations took the view that they had no option but to close their doors or cease activities that had attracted funding in the past. As interviewees explain, given the culture and capacity of the sector, the notion of putting in place contingency plans and seeking out alternative revenues may not come naturally to some organisations.

'You can't generalise, every organisation is different ... but my impression is it is not a very confident sector when it comes to independence from government. It's a case of "right, we must get government to fund this", it's not "people will get behind us on this and they will attend events and give us a bit of help and give us a donation". It is how it has always really done things. The capacity to raise our own money isn't there, the culture to do that isn't there anymore … there is a lack of confidence to say, "we will be doing this anyway, whether you fund it not".' (VCS)

'Maybe we could go back to our [fundraising and participatory] roots a bit, maybe we are too dependent on the [funding] application form.' (VCS)

In line with the idea that the 'new new' is often a mishmash of previous trends, the current 'lack of confidence' within the sector, the despondency in the face of a seemingly chaotic rationalisation, and the failure to actively seek out alternative sources of funding, has echoes of the practices and organisational outlooks that came into play when previous rounds of funding for the sector were being wound down. For example, in the context of a dependency culture that had grown over time between some major funders and VCS grantees, even when there was sufficient prior notification that funding would eventually end, some organisations 'didn't quite believe the reality of spend-down and therefore didn't engage seriously in seeking alternative funds' (Knox and Quirk, 2016, 241). As is the case today, some funding recipients felt 'bereft' and abandoned as final grants came to an end (Knox and Quirk, 2016, 241). Reflecting on the more recent cuts, and the rationalising impulses in government, one official captured the changing mood succinctly by arguing that departments now fund 'organisations to deliver public services and outcomes, not to exist'. In light of this new thinking, other civil servants seem to be suggesting that organisations may cling to cultures and mentalities that were forged in a system that has slowly withered away.

'The [voluntary and community] sector are very stuck in the structures that were there 25 years ago … but if you look at other parts of the world, or industry or whatever, it has all changed, it has changed to reflect the changes in society, but those voluntary and community organisations haven't changed … did people think because they signed a bit of paper in 1998 that that would be it?' (Government official)

'There is an expectation that the existence of organisations will be preserved because they are third sector organisations, rather than because of the role that they are playing.' (Government official)

By specifying '1998', and by suggesting that some organisations believe that they have an inherent value because of their sectoral status, officials may be referencing attitudes and structures that became entrenched during the 1990s and post-agreement funding boom. After the signing of the peace accord in 1998, NI enjoyed a flood of international goodwill, and for decades it had received generous funding for peace programmes. This, in part, had allowed for the rapid growth and professionalisation of the sector (McCall and Williamson, 2001; McCall and O'Dowd, 2008). The woolly and celebratory civil-society discourses that were a characteristic of that time do not figure heavily in the language employed by civil servants, and the changing narratives of government–VCS relationships seem to reflect a view that sections of the sector are a funding-dependent artefact from the peace process era. Whereas during the heyday of the partnership phase in funder–VCS relations some organisations came into being to receive funding, or were sustained because funding was available, government is now beginning to sketch out a new vision for how these relationships will be managed in the future.

These sentiments are also shared by some individuals working in the VCS, most notably among those organisations that feel that they have 'taken their hit' by rationalising, restructuring, formalising collaboration with others and looking to non-government funders for resources. Indeed, some interviewees support and see value in the rationalisation and government–VCS decoupling processes, for they believe it will refresh the independence of the sector and re-channel resources to those most in need. Some go further, suggesting that the times of a 'bloated' funded sector and a 'community development organisation on every corner' should come to an end so that resources can be targeted at those most in need. Some of the interviewees from those organisations that have taken ownership of the rationalisation and reform processes have a strong critique of organisations that, in their view, have failed to adapt to the new climate:

> 'You are a business and you have to be run as a business … times have changed, you have to look beyond central government for funding and collaboration … there needs to be an injection of realism into these discussions now.' (VCS)

Interviewees from the sector explain that, in the past, there was at least a rhetorical commitment to a kind of planned obsolescence, a commitment to the notion that organisations should recognise that they have a shelf life; that they would eventually achieve their goals or make way for others. However, for some interviewees, professionalisation, agentification and a comparatively abnormal funding environment led to a situation where 'zombie' organisations continue to function and access resources, but without delivering identifiable outcomes or innovative practices. As another sectoral interviewee explains, the changing environment means that funders will demand evidence of demonstrable outcomes, thus potentially weeding out some of the more ineffective organisations.

'It isn't good enough for organisations to say we do things that are intangible but are beneficial ... hard economic challenges will pose problems for many organisations, as will the moves towards more outcomes-based funding regimes by trusts and foundations and government ... people are increasingly going to say "we will grant aid you or contract you on the basis of the positive change you achieve in this community". It is going to be harder for the charlatans to hide I would say, but maybe I am being optimistic.' (VCS)

At a time when government is calling for a structural overhaul of the sector and its relationship with the state, for some interviewees it is time to raise and discuss questions around the fundamental nature and role of the sector, questions that the sector may have been unwilling to address in the past.

'Back in the day there was kind of a fundamental position that everyone knew, that "if my organisation was successful, we had to close the doors because we are done". But that has just drifted. I'm not suggesting people did it, but that was just the principled position. I think the position now is that "we are never going to fix this stuff; we need to be funded forever because we are going to be needed".' (VCS)

'Is there a need for all these organisations or are we just fighting for our own jobs ... there are organisations out there and I would ask if they are doing what they were set up to do? I would say not, they just tick the box.' (VCS)

For some interviewees, the new environment needs to be matched by new thinking within government. Those organisations that can be effective and efficient agents in the delivery of government-determined services should be fully supported, while those that cannot deliver should be cut adrift.

> 'Government should determine the service ... and who is needed to deliver that, and well, see the good organisations, fund them. See the bad ones, that aren't doing their job, dump them. Lots of these organisations have mission drift and all. That will cut out a lot of this crap. No department is really prepared to evaluate everything and say "no, you are not performing" ... what they do is a salami cut every time, so it is death by a thousand cuts. So, you are penalising good organisations as well as the bad.' (VCS)

This view is grounded in a recognition of the new environment for government–VCS relationships, and the idea that an organisation must have 'sellable' skills that are the consequence of a longstanding history of delivering outcomes for a specific group of service users. If, as the interviewee suggested on p 84, procurement models are premised on the idea that governments know exactly what they want to buy, then this view may imply that the 'good organisations' will have to acquiesce to top-down agendas and predetermined services. However, the interview data collected with both sectoral and governmental representatives also suggests that, where there is a genuine co-dependency between government and a funded organisation, when an organisation delivers specialist services, it can influence government's agenda and policy implementation in a particular policy field. It seems that some organisations operate in a kind of 'policy community' within which they have become a credible voice through longstanding relationships and a clear ability to evidence results, and government will recognise the VCS's knowledge and expertise in circumstances where its agenda and that of a VCS organisation are in alignment. Therefore, it may be the case that those most confident in their position and expertise will have less concern about an environment that appears to be more instrumentalist and rationalised.

It is clear in the interview data that some participants feel that many organisations have been reluctant to embrace the realities of the new funding environment and the changing relationship between funders and organisations. There is no doubt that recent top-down rationalisations, closures and cuts can seem a quick and ruthless process for an individual organisation that has, as some interviewees suggest, seemingly 'lost funding almost overnight'. However, interviewees also point to how, at a systemic level, the rationalisation process is happening almost in slow motion. As experienced sectoral interviewees explain, there is always just enough funding 'sloshing' around the system to keep at bay a 'sense of urgency' within certain sections of the sector. Other interviewees, echoing the view of some government officials, don't seem to see the failure to adapt to changing circumstances as being driven solely by a Micawberish optimism. As one VCS interviewee suggests:

> 'There is a sense of entitlement out there in many organisations and that is now playing out as a sense of injustice.' (VCS)

These interviewees suggest that a culture of dependency has, over decades, morphed into a 'culture of entitlement', with a sense of privilege now masquerading as a sense of injustice when a funding cut finally arrives.

Returning to the notion that top-down procurement models and the scaling up of contracts promote the development of more simplified and governable partnerships with reduced transaction costs, a theme emerging from the data was the idea that there are calls from government for the sector to engage in a bottom-up process of rationalisation. In these calls, organisations are being urged to merge, collaborate and work in more formalised partnerships. Certainly, this idea of rationalisation is captured in the reflections of officials, and it seems that embracing new forms of organisational structures and collaboration will be key to organisations surviving the new funding environment.

> 'There is a challenge there in harnessing all that is good about the third sector ... it's how you harness that to deliver the outcomes that the various government departments want to achieve but with less resources. So, there is a challenge there for the sector, can the sector step-up, can it rationalise itself.' (Government official)

> 'The organisations have to change, some of them are up for it, some of them aren't. The stronger ones will, the more realistic ones will look to collaborate. Others won't, and that will have consequences for how attractive they are to invest in ... more-switched on groups will see that as an opportunity to merge, to amalgamate, to pick their strengths. The less-switched on ones will go into a competition and fall off the funding line and be in a very difficult position.' (Government official)

However, some sectoral interviewees explain that there is an unrealistic expectation in government that mergers and collaboration will happen organically. According to some sectoral interviewees, there is still too much protectionism of 'personal fiefdoms' and 'empires', a lack of inter-organisational trust, and too much competition between organisations. There is also an unwillingness to have 'difficult conversations' about what the VCS will look like in the future. For some interviewees, government is going to have to take ownership of this rationalisation and work in partnership with the sector to facilitate mergers and collaborations, otherwise government risks losing the structures around which some major strategies will be built. In other words, it is the view of some sectoral interviewees that the preservation of the best aspects of the VCS may require more hierarchical intervention and steering by government in the short term. As some government interviewees acknowledged, at times government policies may inspire competition rather than collaboration, creating a challenging environment for organic and formal collaborations to take place:

> 'It could be that through our funding systems we are introducing more competition when what we actually want to see is more collaboration.' (Government official)

Generally speaking, NI as a region doesn't easily reform and rationalise its governance systems. When NI's post-devolution Review of Public Administration was taken over by the direct-rule administration, 'the focus changed from increasing the accountability of the large quango sector to the devolved administration to rationalisation and cost-cutting', but the UK-wide debate on a 'bonfire of the quangos' didn't get traction in NI and many quangos showed institutional endurance (Birrell and Gormley-Heenan, 2015, 163–4). The often-intractable process of rationalisation in other sectors, where competing interests seek to maintain their position, is now playing out in the VCS. It could also be the case that sectoral frustrations about a seemingly 'chaotic' rationalisation, and their perception of 'unsophisticated cuts', emerge from the fact that the sector and government have unaligned understandings of key ideas. In many ways, the sector still seems to frame the potential of collaboration and networking in terms reminiscent of the 'multiple partners pulling in the same direction' narratives that we would find in optimistic accounts of network governance. It sees collaboration in terms of pragmatic, fluid and flexible responses to complex problems, with responses to these problems being negotiated and decided upon by different interested parties. Celebrating 'collaboration', for government officials and ministers, may be more about engendering a more realistic attitude to the changing financial environment, cost-cutting mergers and bureaucratic rationalisation.

> 'If we went a year or two years ago and talked about collaboration within the voluntary and community sector the minister would have said "how many mergers are there going to be", and I think maybe that attitude still prevails. I would say to them "well, it's more sophisticated than that". Collaboration doesn't mean merger, we are talking about getting lots of people to work together for the benefit of their beneficiaries, and that might mean loads of different models and so on.' (VCS)

Conclusion

As this chapter has illustrated, both the VCS and government officials are seeking to adjust to and manage the winding down of a decades-long 'boom' period for the VCS in NI. Due to a policy direction that began under conflict-era direct-rule administrations, and that accelerated under New Labour, the VCS had enjoyed waves of financial and rhetorical support from government and other funders. It was the beneficiary of strategies that sought to reinforce government–VCS partnerships, and the mainstreaming of the sector in governance, service delivery, peacebuilding, community relations programmes and community development. As was suggested in previous chapters, the New Labour era in particular was experienced as a period of 'stability and growth' by many voluntary organisations (see Hemmings, 2017, 52), whereas the more punitive form of neoliberalism being pursued by the Conservative Party since 2010, has seen many VCS organisations finding themselves in a difficult financial position during a period of government–VCS decoupling. As this chapter has illustrated, similar processes of decoupling, rationalisation, instrumentalism and reform are now playing out in NI.

As we have seen in previous chapters, the New Labour project was concerned with managing some of the more socially erosive effects of markets and competitive individualism on social cohesion and stability, and the sector was a perfect site for rolling out communitarian ideas concerning the value of a cooperative and consensual 'partnership ethos' (Davies, 2009, 88), social capital, collaboration and network building. However, this chapter has also illustrated how the sector has been a key part of the neoliberal practice of co-opting civil-society institutions, and using these institutions as a site for rolling out and normalising other 'appropriate' neoliberal norms and worldviews around the value of competition, efficiency and self-help. However, as has been hinted at already, and as we shall see in future chapters, this is far from being a completed project, for interviewees continue to problematise narratives and practices that celebrate competition, efficiency and 'the market'. We have also seen that the claims to a collaborative ethos may have less explanatory power than is suggested in the orthodox narrative put forward by government and the sectoral bureaucracy. In NI, the virtuous circle of cooperation that is described by communitarian theorists looks more like a zigzagged line of funding-mandated relationships and 'cooperation by default'. Even if a cooperative ethos had been instilled through these mandated partnerships, it seems that this ethos cannot bear the weight that is put on it by the antagonisms that arise out of organisational competition and territorialism. As we shall see in the next chapter, sectoral competition, its enrolment into neoliberal projects, the chaotic decoupling from government and the long history of government–VCS partnerships are related to and overlap with broader concerns around sectoral independence.

FIVE

Independence of voice, purpose and action

As noted in previous chapters, recent changes in the government–VCS relationship have ignited yet another round of debates about the sector's independence, its distinctiveness vis-à-vis other sectors, and its relationship with the state (Acheson, 2013; Panel on the Independence of the Voluntary Sector, 2014; Ketola and Hughes, 2016). Of course, defining both the independence and distinctiveness of the VCS is not an easy task (Macmillan, 2012) for it is a 'loose and baggy monster' (Kendall and Knapp, 1995; Alcock, 2010) made up of a myriad of organisational types and sizes. The VCS conducts its work in many policy fields, its organisations have a range of geographical remits and each organisation has a particular relationship with government and other funders. This means that experiences and understandings of independence are likely to be as varied as the sector is diverse. Despite the complexity of the issue, and with no agreed understanding of what is meant by independence, across the UK some sectoral actors recognised that there was a need to 'start the debate somewhere', and that mechanisms were needed for exploring the sector's relationship with government and threats to its independence.

These debates have covered, inter alia, issues around the 'contract culture', threats to the sector's purportedly distinctive culture and values, top-down bureaucracy, contract prescriptiveness, 'mission drift', state co-option, government–VCS consultation and lobbying, campaigning and 'independence of voice'. In both the UK and internationally, this wide-ranging debate on the future of the sector was confronting how a shifting policy environment, and organisational responses to this new environment, had the potential to impact on the claimed ethos and nature of the sector. There have also been many debates and discussions on the different traditions of VCS action and the role of the sector in explicitly political activities, such as campaigning for improved and accountable universal public services and social protections (see NCIA, 2015). In many ways NI's VCS has been catching up to its counterparts in other regions in that it is facing similar issues in terms of its independence. However, as was suggested in the previous chapters, and as will become clearer in the following sections, for a long time the level of debate about the role and nature of the VCS, its independence, and the nature of its relationship with government, has lagged behind the debate being held elsewhere.

Independence of purpose and action

The ability of organisations to stay true to their mission and values in a funding environment that has become increasingly instrumental and competitive has been central to recent debates on sectoral independence. Central themes in the interview data were the issue of 'mission drift' and the prioritisation of organisational survival over a commitment to one's founding mission. According to many interviewees, making and implementing the difficult decisions that would allow an organisation to stay aligned with its founding principles and mission, and making decisions according to purported sectoral values like 'freedom of action', are being postponed as organisational survival becomes the priority.

> 'I have said to staff in here, my advice is to look for another job, because I have known that the only way to keep them on is by doing things that go against why we exist ... I think, perhaps, a number of organisations have forgotten that the reason you exist is your voice, purpose and action.' (VCS)

As we have seen in previous chapters, there is a growing view that in the new environment for government–VCS relationships, there should be little tolerance for this 'mission drift' and keep the organisation open at all costs mentality. Some CDWs go further, suggesting that competition between organisations, the contradictions inherent to a professionalised sector that is funded by government, and the dominance of a 'follow the money' attitude, raises questions about the values and norms that drive practices in today's VCS. Some see sectoral organisations' missions shifting according to the latest round of available funding or the policy priorities of the day, while others argue that there is a need to discuss how the funding environment and professionalisation have shaped the principles and priorities of the sector.

> 'Independence is lovely in theory, but it is very expensive ... we have always sought to keep independent thought in our minds and not change our ideas and our principles ... but it is very difficult when there are resources there, and I've seen so many people, they will say they aren't, but they are actually changing

according to the money, or changing course according to the policies of a particular time.' (VCS)

'Some organisations have followed the money; some organisations have exploited the money but managed to stay fairly true to their aims. But it would be interesting to look at the heart and soul of community development in particular and see where it's at. When community development started in the 1960s there was a lot of naivety and hippie-dom around it, but yet the core principles were right. Are they still there? And I mean that as, in inverted commas, a "professional community worker". Isn't that a contradiction in terms nearly? The funding environment over the last ten to fifteen years has informed that to some degree. So, I think there needs to be some discussion around that.' (VCS)

Some interviewees suggest that funders have slowly become more 'savvy', and are less willing to fund organisations that cannot evidence impact or display a real and historical connection with a service-user group. If this is the case, constantly shifting the organisation's mission to simply sustain its existence may no longer be an option. However, in a period of chaotic rationalisation and funding cuts, mistakes will be made by both funders and organisations, and with the quest for organisational survival being the priority, it can sometimes be the case that organisations find themselves in a difficult position as they try to align their mission with available funding streams. As one funding body official notes:

'Organisations have found themselves in difficulties as they try to fit round pegs in square holes.' (Funding body official)

Key to understanding issues such as mission drift, or the issue of organisations operating to a 'predetermined script', is a recognition that government, to a significant degree, determines the financial, discursive and political context within which organisations exist. Government determines the funding landscape and policy priorities, and organisations may try to fit within this system. Assembly committees and government departments may have urged public bodies and sectoral organisations to renew their efforts to adhere to the principles of the concordat, but in general, the data collected as part of this research showed less evidence of the 'equitable partners' narratives that had dominated policy language for decades. In the new discourses of government–VCS relationships being articulated by

Westminster, discourses that are echoed by NI officials and in policy documentation, it seems that organisations will have to align their objectives even more closely with government objectives if they are to survive the 'tighter public-funding environment'. Government officials recognise that this will raise difficult issues for sector organisations as regards their independence and mission.

'We have moved more to a service-delivery model, we are prescribing the outcomes ... what does that mean for the independence of the sector? I don't know, because we will be saying look, we want you to be doing A, B, C and D, for us. Now, does doing A, B, C and D mean you are not really independent from us, you are just an agent, and where does the challenge go? Do bits of the sector feel confident to say "no we don't want to do that"?'(Government official)

This view also echoes the questions raised in the previous sections by sectoral interviewees, particularly in terms of how 'confident' sector organisations would be in moving towards a situation where they exit restrictive partnership arrangements, look elsewhere for financing and support and conduct their activities independently from government. The instrumentalist approach to the sector being described by officials, the shift away from core funding towards the financing of specific predetermined services, is certainly a challenge for some organisations in terms of protecting their independence. The comments of sectoral interviewees reflect broad concerns about 'freedom of action' in the VCS more generally.

'Independence of the charity is really, really important to us as an organisation ... before, [government] funders would invest in the organisation, in the core, and the board would determine the needs of the charity ... what are the needs of our clients and so on ... [with changes in the funding structures] they want to contract the charity to do particular things for them.' (VCS)

Whereas in the past there were promises from government that asymmetries in power would be addressed, the views expressed by officials suggest greater recognition of the fact that, in practice, it is difficult to reconcile the differences in power between a VCS organisation and a government funder. There may be top-down rhetorical support for a distinct sphere of independent voluntary and community action that is supported through diverse financial sources and voluntarism. However, there seems to be more openness about the fact that government's decision-making processes, as regards the government-funded sector, will be driven by top-down procurement priorities, prescriptive outcomes and budgetary concerns. In addition, a number of officials would seem to suggest that claims to independence were always a little exaggerated.

> 'To some extent their [the funded sector's] independence is curtailed, because when you get into a project or programme or arrangement with government, whatever part of government it is, it will have various conditions and it will set those conditions … that is a challenge for the sector and the officials involved, to find a middle way that delivers what government wants, and to some extent doesn't compromise the sector.' (Government official)

As Coule and Bennett (2018, 154S) have suggested, 'the issues vexing the Panel on the Independence of the Voluntary Sector', including instrumentalism, co-option and restrictions on campaigning, 'troubled the Deakin Commission almost 20 years previous and can be traced back further to Wolfenden in 1978'. These discussions are far from new, even though the intensity with which these issues are playing out may be different when compared to previous eras. However, as government officials may be hinting at, there are grounds for scepticism over any of the more recent 'moral panics' about independence, particularly when that panic coincides with a restructuring of financial arrangements between the VCS, government and other funders. Indeed, some officials seem to greet the sectoral rumblings about independence and governmental 'control freakery' with bemusement. For these officials, issues of independence never troubled the VCS in the past and, therefore, a move to a more explicitly prescriptive and technocratic form of funding should not be overly concerning for those that can successfully align their mission with government objectives.

> 'I don't think the sector has made its case for its independence, they have drifted along on this stream of central-government funding and European funding … it's a case of "Europe will pay us to do this or that, so that is what we are going to do", but whether that is what you started out doing 20 years ago doesn't seem to matter.' (Government official)

Now that the period of massive 'international goodwill' towards the region has come to an end, and the substantial amounts of resources for investment in 'developing civil society' have been expended, it may be the case that what government and other funders are willing to finance has become narrower and more prescribed. However, in many ways, this has just narrowed the scope for organisations to position themselves as agents in the delivery of a predetermined service or programme, and, as many interviewees suggest, there are real question marks around the capacity for the sector to be a site of innovative practice in such an environment. Some organisations have made small acts of resistance against state co-option, the 'chasing-the-money' culture and the ethos that prioritises organisational survival and empire building. In some instances, this will involve making a 'cost-benefit analysis' on a case-by-case basis, with organisations choosing to refuse a particular funder or contract if they feel it would overly compromise their independence or ways of working with their service users. For example, one interviewee explained that their organisation took a stand against becoming agents in a project which, in their view, was more concerned with 'massaging statistics' than with dealing with the underlying causes of poverty and unemployment in their working-class community.

> '[With some funding streams and programmes] you design your programme ... and as long as you meet your targets, which you would want to meet anyway, you are left to your own devices for your methods ... [some funding streams and programmes] are very prescriptive, that you have to deliver in a particular way ... you have to make choices about these things, don't just chase the money if you're not happy with the method of whatever they are wanting to fund.' (VCS)

> 'There is almost always a conflict between the expectations of the funder, especially if its government, and what activists on the ground know will work. For instance, I have personal experience of programmes that were government funded, and the expectation would be that our organisation would take them on. But we refused. The programme was useless, and so we resisted that. People would say, "how can you do that, this is an opportunity for local people", but it wasn't, it was about massaging statistics, you know. So, we looked elsewhere.' (VCS)

Austerity, mission drift and sectoral 'opportunities'

As the VCS has become increasingly dependent on 'funding derived from the provision of erstwhile public services' (Knox and Quirk,

2016, 17), the recent rounds of austerity and cuts have put back into focus not just issues of sectoral funding dependency, but also perennial questions around the VCS's role in potentially eroding and fragmenting universal welfare services (see Popple and Redmond, 2000, 398). We need to bear in mind that state retrenchment is not always a negative from the sector's point of view. It creates 'opportunities' for the VCS, with state withdrawal leaving in its wake unaddressed needs that justify the existence and funding of VCS organisations (Herman and Yarwood, 2015, 2642). However, as the NCIA (2015, 1) argued during its campaign on sectoral independence, many responsibilities in the area of social need and protections 'must rest with the state' because VCS organisations 'are neither universal nor democratically accountable'. Echoing this sentiment, and reflecting an issue that is closely related to mission drift and organisational survival, some sectoral interviewees believe that organisations are using the 'rush for funding' as a justification for taking on services that may not necessarily belong in the sector. In doing so, these organisations are handing government an opportunity to transfer responsibilities away from the state and down to the VCS and communities. As a number of interviewees suggest, organisations will take on responsibilities in return for some (initial) funding, but they may not have fully thought through the implications of taking on a service that properly belongs in a democratically accountable public body that is staffed by permanent, and often unionised, workers.

The monopsonistic conditions that are characteristic of many government–VCS relationships mean that the state has control over the price it will pay partners for a service, and hence control over the nature and quality of that service. In the UK more broadly, in a context in which there is intense competition for funding and massive governmental control over the price and nature of services, there has been a 'race to the bottom' environment within which staff wages are deprioritised (Living Wage Foundation, 2018, 1). In essence, in some parts of the UK's VCS, very precarious workers now serve very precarious populations (DeVerteuil, 2017, 1527), and according to many interviewees, the same arguments could apply to NI's VCS. This precarity at the lower levels is happening amid intermittent public and media focus on excessive chief executive pay levels, damaging financial mismanagement scandals and concerns about fundraising practices, all of which have taken their toll on the overall 'stock of the voluntary sector' (Hemmings, 2017, 42). Unsurprisingly, therefore, there are questions from within the VCS concerning not just its role in taking on services that might be better delivered by accountable state bodies, but its social-justice credentials more broadly.

'Sometimes things go wrong and you're actually advocating for stuff that isn't practised [in the VCS] ... do they [VCS organisations] actually have paid maternity leave, there's lots of places don't, pensions, they don't. So that kind of is a difficulty, because they are running on a shoestring, but it is not actually a good enough excuse, for me anyway, so I just find that dichotomy very strange.' (VCS)

'It looks like this sector is delivering public services cheaper than the public sector ... do you want your public services delivered by the public sector, in which workers are given strong unionised positions, decent pensions, good terms and conditions, holidays and all the rest of it? Or would you prefer if that service is delivered by this sector, but by people who in the main are women in part-time jobs that are comparatively poorly paid ... it tends to be part-time women [workers] who need the flexibility, you know ... and they can be easily disposed of.' (VCS)

As we have already seen, interviewees from across the sector believe that government perceives VCS activities as peripheral, even when it is at the forefront of dealing with entrenched problems in Northern Irish society, or when it is working with some of its most marginalised communities. This sense that the VCS's work is seen in the corridors of power as peripheral makes the dependence on government resources, the lack of alternative sources of funding and the transfer of responsibilities away from the state even more concerning for some interviewees.

'Whenever cuts come, and there is going to be more, you [those in the VCS] are going to be the first that gets it, because what we do is never going to be a priority. It is never going to be a priority to fix mental health or to work with travellers or whatever. So, when you are reliant on government funding for that work, you are in a really seriously precarious position.' (VCS)

For many interviewees, this transfer of risk and responsibilities away from the state is even more concerning in light of recent policy discourses concerning the role of volunteers and 'community' in the delivery of services, as opposed to paid staff. As noted in Chapter Two, under the Coalition and Conservative governments, many organisations have been relegated to unpaid community work, and in Westminster, a dependent VCS 'mini public sector' was seen as 'crowding out' spontaneous social action. This view is echoed in the reflections of some officials, and as in the wider UK, it seems that decision makers are beginning to look closely at how the funded VCS has the potential to act as a barrier to the development of spontaneous voluntary and community action:

> 'When we set these [funded programmes] up, we create a dependency ... in an area of strained resources, we paradoxically might be crowding out volunteering through our policies.' (Government official)

Both the subtle and more obvious shifts in policy rhetoric, and the 'discourses of scarcity' that are central to the analysis of the financial environment by governments (and, indeed, some sectoral interviewees), would suggest that there could be a renewed emphasis on developing structures for unpaid voluntary action, with sectoral volunteers filling vacuums left by the state's withdrawal.

> 'Society depends on public money, so there has to be a change in society that things that were maybe done by government and through the public sector could well be done on a voluntary basis ... it doesn't mean government steps back, but it does mean it could put in an infrastructure that is populated by volunteers ... activities ... could be provided on a voluntary basis by the community, and the voluntary sector could organise that.' (Government official)

In light of earlier discussions around the fact that the VCS has both professionalised and undergone decades of isomorphic changes, it is increasingly seen as just one player among many in a competitive environment. In this context, it may only be perceived by decision makers as bringing a distinctive 'added value' if it can mobilise free labour in the form of volunteers. As officials explain, the sector's pay structures are in line with the public sector, and as we have already seen, the 'dog-eat-dog' competition and protectionism is more akin to private-sector practices. Though there is undoubtedly recognition of the VCS's role in areas where there is state or market failure, and although some officials do see the VCS as the preferred provider of services that require local or specialist knowledge, the interview data did not capture a clear articulation of what could be regarded as sectoral 'distinctiveness'.

'I wonder if the sector are emphasising enough the volunteering part of their role … often when we are engaging with them it is about the contracting of a delivery of a service and they want to be paid for that service, but in that respect they are the same as a commercial provider, or in fact a public provider, and their pay policies reflect the public sector usually, so what's the advantage then, you would have to say.' (Government official)

Echoing the 'mini public sector' critique of Westminster, in contrast to the notion of a sector that is funded directly by the state to deliver services, some officials conceptualise the VCS as a structure that will enable volunteerism and social responsibility. Some sectoral interviewees recognise that the idea of volunteers taking on the role and activities of professional staff is gaining traction within government circles. However, for these interviewees, volunteers cannot match the services provided by professional and trained staff, and as volunteering is freely given labour, a reliance on volunteers would mean a breakdown in the hierarchy and order within the organisation. Some see the focus on volunteering as being driven by efforts to pressure organisations to do more with less, and by an ideological commitment to shrinking government spending. For many interviewees, any focus in government on filling gaps with volunteers is based on a fundamental misunderstanding of both volunteering as a practice and the capacity of volunteers. In the view of multiple sectoral interviewees, government's celebration of the volunteering aspect of the VCS can be boiled down to the idea that services can be delivered in the sector 'on the cheap'.

'I am all for promoting volunteers, we couldn't open the doors in the morning without volunteers … government think they can get everything done for shit, but volunteers need coordination, they need to feel they are part of something, they need to feel they are doing something of value, not only that they are giving, but that they feel part of a team. That means that there has to be coordination, and that has to be paid for … [volunteering] is not about getting something done for nothing, but I think that's often the way government thinks about it.' (VCS)

An independent voice?

As previous chapters have illustrated, the VCS still sees itself as a connected and influential agent of change in Northern Irish society, and despite the decades of close government–VCS relationships and funding dependency, government also continues to be a cheerleader in the representation of the VCS as strong, critical and campaigning (DSD, 2011). In recent years, it has been suggested that VCS advocacy, campaigning and 'independence of voice' have been under threat, not least out of a fear of 'biting the hand that feeds it' as it has increasingly moved into a service-delivery role (Acheson, 2009; Panel on the Independence of the Voluntary Sector, 2014). Issues around independence, advocacy and resource dependency were certainly key themes in the data collected with sectoral interviewees. As they explain, when there is a reliance on government funding, and when organisations have moved into service-delivery roles, there is an understandable fear that funding, jobs and services could potentially be lost if an organisation were to be critical of government. Within the VCS, and even within a single organisation, there can be tensions and disagreements over the issue of challenging government and campaigning against policy decisions.

'They [VCS organisations] are compromised ... the reality is that is where they have been placed by government policy, in very much of a service-provider role, depending on what government decides is their policy of the day ... it is basically a power relationship and they [government] are the funder, you know, and maybe the challenging role that they did more of before ... that has kind of diminished by necessity.' (VCS)

'We have an interesting board, where we have half who would just be "let's just do community development and that will be lovely", and the other half would be saying "where is our role in resisting welfare reform et cetera" ... our thing is paid for by the department, and there is different energies in here about a willingness to bite the hand that's feeding you, you know. So we wrestle with that.' (VCS)

Echoing the view of those interviewees who see an ethos of empire building driving sectoral practices in the areas of funding competition, inter-organisational collaboration and information sharing, some interviewees involved in policy and campaigning suggest that the same ethos has created a set of unspoken rules around sectoral lobbying and campaigning practices. In order to protect the 'empire', organisations must appear grateful for the access and finances given to them by government, and not do anything that would disrupt this relationship.

'There is a lot of fat cats getting high salaries ... people are empire building, they want to create their own wee empire and they want to keep that empire. So, for you to be involved you have to play the game. It [the government–VCS relationship] is very much like an unequal marriage ... you have to be grateful and just go "thanks very much, that's great" and make sure you don't bite the hand that feeds you.' (VCS)

The finances and programmes that brought about funding dependency, professionalisation and political quiescence in the VCS are seen by many interviewees to be part of a deliberate strategy by government to co-opt and silence potential critics and dissenters:

'That [service-delivery role] has been a very deliberate government policy, because it has completely cut down the levels of challenge in those organisations.' (VCS)

As the data in previous sections suggests, in more recent years organisations in the VCS have recognised that austerity was an opportunity for government to both financially decouple from portions of the VCS and streamline its relationships with the sector. Some organisational leaders recognise their precarious position in terms of being critical of government in this environment, and they suggest that key decision makers now have less patience for those that are seen as being potentially troublesome.

'You have to remember they [government] are paying your salary, and don't be overly critical of them because ... that is the other big difference today, I do think that government departments and particular civil servants are more ruthless about just pulling the plug.' (VCS)

During the period of austerity-driven cuts, some organisations did actively campaign against what they perceived as government's efforts to simplify and centralise services. However, among those that did take action, there is recognition that certain sections of the sector will have been reticent in critiquing a loss in funding lest it threaten future opportunities. In this interviewee's view, there has also been a shift in the VCS's culture and skills base away from agonistic practices.

'During the cuts ... we didn't want to go down with a whimper and we were strong enough to survive it ... we were aware that there would be some people who wouldn't be happy we were making a stand ... in terms of future funding, perhaps that [making a public stand] would be an issue for some groups ... organisations did go to the wall and close down and they didn't even make a whimper. I wouldn't blame protest on not getting funding. Austerity, and where you fit in the funding game, many other reasons than protesting, will explain why you don't get funding ... people are not as good at protest as they used to be.' (VCS)

According to interviewees, one way of protecting the agonistic role of the sector is ensuring that an organisation has access to diverse funding sources. A 'funding mix', which combines contracts, grants and more 'social enterprise' activities, allows organisations to retain their independence, particularly when it seeks to challenge the decisions of policymakers.

'We have lots of contracts with government to deliver particular things, and I've no problem with that ... but to protect ourselves and retain our independence the most important thing we can do is make sure we build up multi-faceted funding sources of government contracts, private-sector trust funds and private donations, events and income generation ... to be able to go to the departments and have a challenging role on a particular policy area you need that independence, but that's a challenge for everybody.' (VCS)

However, even this strategy for protecting independence of voice, and the organisation's advocacy role, may have implications for the nature of the sector in the future. As some interviewees suggest, as independence came to be determined by the diversity of an organisation's funding sources, the 'skill set' that they need to attract to their board has changed, with financial, business, research and other technical competencies being the criteria for inclusion on a board. Although further research in NI is needed, it would be important to explore the knock-on effect of such a recruitment policy, for it could raise questions around the class and social background of board members, and have implications for the diversity and inclusiveness of governance and leadership within the sector (see Inclusive Boards, 2018).

The data would suggest that funding dependency, and a fear of 'biting the hand that feeds', can to some extent explain the perceived political quiescence of the sector, and the sense that it has lost some of its capacity to be a change agent in Northern Irish society (see McKinney, 2017). However, the data also suggests that when we explore the sector's reluctance to challenge government's policy directions, focusing solely on funding dependence will tell only a partial story. Rather, we need to understand how these stories of political quiescence and reticence reflect a complex mix of overlapping social, historical and political processes that have shaped the sector and its role in Northern Irish society. For example, as regards this view that 'people are not as good at protest as they used to be', we need to remember that during the conflict the VCS was the natural home for those individuals that wanted to participate in the political life of the region, but who also felt alienated from the divisive and ethno-sectarian nature of party politics in NI (Cochrane, 2000). However, many interviewees believe that the wider population and younger generations would now tend to see the VCS in much the same way as they would any other industry – as an essentially depoliticised sphere of society that offers employment opportunities.

'I don't see the same energy coming up among young people. They tend to look to the [voluntary and] community sector for jobs and they see it as a career, whereas I think a lot of community development, particularly here in the city, was from a social background.' (VCS)

'There are people who are attracted to working in the [voluntary and community] sector … but the sector isn't attracting the campaigners, let's say, it is attracting people who see it as a job, a professional job.' (VCS)

It is worth remembering that during the Troubles, the British government pursued an 'acceptable-level-of-violence' policy (Morrow, 2017), and in part this involved efforts to grow a politically and culturally ambiguous middle class through the creation of publicly funded jobs (Shirlow and Murtagh, 2006). In a view that calls to mind this insight, one experienced activist raises the question as to whether the VCS may have been used by government as another site for the implementation of this class-building strategy. For another interviewee, the decades of funding dependency and increasing professionalisation means that the tradition of VCS activity that is grounded in having a 'critical and radical edge' must coexist with that part of the sector that developed into funding-dependent service-delivery organisations.

'In many ways government policy over the last 30 or 40 years has been, through the public sector, to create a class, a middle class, that would not become involved in violent conflict. And I firmly believe that. The civil service became so big here because it was a way of government drawing people out of their communities, and it was made into permanent secure work so they wouldn't become involved in radical violence and whatever. So, they created this middle class who in any other society wouldn't be sustainable. Is the sector outside of that system now?' (VCS)

'There are still some parts of the [voluntary and community] sector that are radical enough ... it definitely has professionalised but I hope, and I know, that some organisations have kept their critical kind of edge ... I can honestly say that there is going to be a need for government to fund some part of the sector, it is really, really important. At the same time, I think that any organisation that is completely reliant on that kind of funding is mad. If you are in that position you do absolutely lose your critical edge.' (VCS)

We also need to bear in mind that the traditional political parties may have become more acceptable in the eyes of more of the population, and for those on the progressive or Left wing of the political spectrum, new vehicles for political activism have emerged in the form of new political parties and movements that sit outside the traditional VCS. As one interviewee suggests, in the sector 'you just get a job' in a given organisation and 'you move up the ranks', and the movement of individuals within and between the VCS and the public sector would suggest that it is largely a site for individuals to take on technocratic and managerial roles within the different layers of governance and service delivery. It is not, as interviewees suggested, looked upon as being the natural site for activism that is grounded in a commitment to a particular issue or theory of change. It is also important to remember that the VCS's role in Northern Irish society had been consolidated over time by a longstanding and largely unchallenged narrative about the sector's 'intrinsic value' as a partner of government in peacebuilding and service delivery, and that its relationship with government was moulded into its current form during the New Labour 'partnership' era. This third-way imagining of civil society owed much more to the communitarian idea that community and the sector could be a free or low-cost provider of services than it did 'to more radical visions of participatory democracy' (Corcoran, 2017, 287). This partnership model also implied certain norms of behaviour, and privileged consensus building and non-disruptive discussion with one's partners in government.

'The relationship with government has been about partnership, which hasn't really suited the [voluntary and community] sector, because when it [government] does make the cuts it's a friendly conversation afterwards, you don't go out on the streets ... government knows it can make these decisions and there will be a wee bit of hubbub ... but it's a case of we go to our friend [government] and say this and this happened, it's not a case of "how dare you do this". That is where the lack of independence is evident. They can cut across the board and there will be very little resistance to it at all. The organisations that are hit, most will close and be quiet about it.' (VCS)

As another VCS interviewee suggests:

'In my view there has been too much partnership ... there isn't any of the creative chaos that the sector should be.' (VCS)

In many ways, the decades of formalised civil society–government interaction, the partnership agenda and sectoral access to the corridors of power have made certain theories of change particularly influential within the VCS. There is a belief that the expertise of 'insider-outsiders' can be fed into the decision-making system, and there is a commitment to the idea that logical evidence-based argument can persuade and influence decision makers. Antagonistic tactics should be deployed sparingly and as a last resort, with relationship building and persuasion being the most powerful weapons in the VCS's armoury.

'Voluntary organisations should not simply be parties of protest ... when you are on the streets and you are protesting against something the government has done you have already lost a lot of the ground in the argument, it's really the last stage. When you are in a position when you are trying to influence them, you have got to think about how you build a relationship with them and persuade them to take on policies and show them the evidence ... on the other hand, if you are not being listened to, there comes a time when you need to be more robust, but I would rather be in the business of persuading.' (VCS)

It seems that, just as in the wider UK, there was widespread sectoral buy-in to the 'partnership ethos' espoused in the third-way ideology that drove partnership and network governance discourses and practices in the 1990s and 2000s (see Davies, 2011a). Now that the other aspects of the neoliberal imagining of the role of the VCS are playing out in full, with reduced resources available in many service areas and a renewed focus on unpaid labour, some interviewees feel that decades of government–VCS partnership building and 'insider' professionalised advocacy has left the sector ill-prepared for an environment where antagonistic and conflictual relationships with government might be more appropriate. In the past, significant external funders may have provided some organisations with the capacity to 'challenge the status quo through radical thinking' and evidence-led advocacy (Knox and Quirk, 2016, 261–2). However, the sector has also been fed 'on a diet of government and EU funding' (Knox and Quirk, 2016, 261–2), and partnership and multi-level governance arrangements and discourses were very influential in this funding milieu. As the interviewees' comments suggest, this has nudged groups in the direction of eschewing conflict with their departmental patrons in favour of vertical partnership and collaboration, relationship building, consultation mechanisms and insider efforts at 'persuasion' within government's invited spaces. However, given the imbalances of power, it is easy to see why some may feel that even the most prominent VCS voices struggle to become any more than an 'accommodated noise'. It is also easy to see why, for many activists, all this consultation, all the meetings, all the time and resources invested, are part of a cynical attempt by government to keep the sector busy and 'numbed'.

'The last thing they [government] have the time or interest to do is to listen to the voluntary and community sector … there are [VCS] agencies that have some clout, but you have to wonder is it effective clout or just an accommodated noise. You know, it's "come and talk to us … right that's very interesting, think we agree with ya. Bye!"' (VCS)

'This drives me up the walls, responding to policy consultations is not a critical part of the voluntary sector, that is a waste of time. Once quality impact assessments came in, and consultations, and then the new buzz words like "consultation fatigue", and all the going to meetings. It is just a way of keeping the sector numbed. There are people paid big money and that is what they do – respond to consultations all the time.' (VCS)

'The amount to which it [participation in invited spaces] can become influential is really, really limited ... the government has the ability, democratic government has the ability, to look like everyone is being listened to, and it will even instigate its own channels, but it has a way of absorbing what it hears from those channels.' (VCS)

These sentiments also reflect the ways in which the VCS has become embedded in a system that discursively and practically positions it as a technocratic service provider (Carmel and Harlock, 2008, 155), and the ways in which neoliberal governance has been concerned with the creation of an unnavigable buffer zone between the citizen and the state that is made up of elite-recognised stakeholders and experts. As suggested in Chapter One, within these spaces, politics gives way to policy (Swyngedouw, 2009, 609), and discussions revolve around technocratic concerns and 'expert' administration. As interviewees explain, the makeup of events, meetings and governance spaces now reflects this recognition of professionalised stakeholders, and the messages articulated by the most influential voices reflect the interests of larger organisations that can operate and survive in this technocratic environment.

'When you go into a meeting or an event now, it is three quarters men in suits, businessmen, who I do not know ... when years ago, and this is really true, everybody was wearing jeans and jumpers. The whole face of people, the whole face of the sector has changed, because it's not the community and the voluntary, it's the big service providers.' (VCS)

'I think there is a big divergence between what's happening on the ground and what's been put across to government and I think very often the big infrastructure organisations, I suppose for very good reasons, but they get to where the people that are making demands on them tend to be the bigger organisations who have very clear messages that they want to get across and then it's very easy to support a very clear message. I think they also get quite often into the technicalities. So that government, if you like, create the narrative and they work within that narrative and tweak it.' (VCS)

'It's the same cabal that turn up at everything, and I know, having sat in enough of them [meetings], they make the same points ad nauseam. Valid or not, you know what they are going to say ... we [the VCS] are part of that fraternity ... we live in the same environment and no one will rock the boat ... we are all legitimate in the eyes of the state. We co-exist.' (VCS)

Though funding was supposed to be about building up the capacity of the sector to have an independent and critiquing voice as part of a process of democratic renewal, and even though this was an explicitly stated goal with regards to some non-state funding, even some officials seem to be bemoan the lack of alternative visions being articulated by the sector and its overly reactive response to the policy environment within which it operates.

'I think the intention has always been, in our funding, to be able to give the sector money in order for it to have that independent voice, but I don't think they use that opportunity very well, I don't think they know how to engage with government ... they don't have a vision for the future, it's all reactive.' (Government official)

It is important to remember that throughout the third-way era, neoliberal governments had relatively fixed boundaries around what policy responses were deemed acceptable or feasible in areas that the VCS was centrally involved in. In such a policymaking environment, and even if otherwise inclined, a civil-society actor would have to restrict itself to picking at the margins of policy implementation if it wished to maintain its status as a credible voice within the policy community. In a similar vein, it was more likely for the sector to argue for more 'joined-up' inter-agency working to address an issue within a specific client-group, than it was for the sector to lobby for a relatively straightforward universal or redistributive policy response. With the VCS becoming a site for employment for the credentialed middle-class, and with its role in multi-level partnerships and governance spaces, the sector became an administrator of a suite of Rube Goldberg machine 'anti-poverty' and social exclusion policies and technocratic fixes that were unthreatening to middle-class interests. It was to the technicalities of these policies and programmes that its attention was drawn.

Finally, the organisational convergence towards a political space of 'lowest-common-denominator' technocracy reflects decades-long efforts to bring together organisations with disparate and conflicting worldviews into a sectoral 'big tent', for a discourse of unity would help secure the sector's 'political profile, policy support and financial backing' (Alcock, 2010, 19). This project had both localised and UK-wide dimensions. At the UK level, an alliance of sectoral representatives, policymakers, political actors and researchers were promoting the notion of a 'unifying ideology of a third sector' (Alcock, 2010, 19) that would iron out some of the tensions and differences in the sector, and this process coincided with New Labour's 'partnership agenda' and discourses. At the local level, some community activist approaches and traditions would have been seen as inappropriately anti-state in Protestant communities (see Kilmurray, 2017, 193). For example, a CDW working within a Protestant working-class area explained that 'community development' would have been viewed with suspicion in the loyalist community because it was seen as having associations with the republican agenda. Another interviewee from a working-class Protestant area, reflecting on the VCS infrastructure within Protestant communities and the important role of the church, explained that there was always a tendency to align organisations with the general thrust of establishment policy.

'There was more passivity on the part of the Protestant and disadvantaged working classes really ... the challenge is that in the Protestant churches, it has been very close with, very aligned politically and in social outlook, with the civil service ... in the upstanding pillars of governance the churches were in there ... there was that whole range of alignment with the system and so there was very little energy for critique ... there has not been a strong critique of government emerging from the Protestant community with regard to disadvantage ... and the church really struggles to be an advocate for the working classes.' (VCS)

In such a context, collective sectoral buy-in to narratives of government–VCS partnership, and the prioritisation of a communitarian 'small-c conservative' imagining of community development and voluntary action made sense. As in the UK more broadly, narratives of voluntary action that revolved around 'partnership' and technocratic centrism secured the VCS's role in governance and its financial backing, but in NI they also helped allow sectoral coalitions from across the main political cleavages to function in a relatively uncontroversial fashion. Each organisational leadership was then free to imagine their organisation as embodying whatever mix of VCS traditions best reflected their worldview, theory of change and organisational practices.

Conclusion

Throughout much of NI's troubled history, the VCS has been afforded a privileged role in the governance of the region. Its position was secured by the development of close relationships between VCS elites, civil servants and funding bodies, a huge flow of resources into its coffers and a narrative that celebrated the VCS as the 'glue holding society together'. However, in an increasingly instrumental policy environment, there are now real questions around the extent to which the VCS can be seen as offering any meaningful contribution that is independent from government. In the context of the sector's buy-in to agendas and discourses that have seen it largely co-opted by the state, and in the context where there are so many barriers against the VCS's articulation of alternative visions, it seems that the sector has become a site where government's neoliberal agenda is enabled rather than resisted (Hughes, 2019). In many ways this is an odd conclusion, given that many sectoral interviewees put forward a nuanced analysis of the region's neoliberal and technocratic policies, and insightful reflections on the effects of these policies on the role and nature of the region's VCS and working-class communities. The issues explored in this chapter are far from being specific to NI. Sectoral organisations across the UK may be exploring how they can pragmatically 'play the funding game', but at the same time hold on to some of their 'unruly, grassroots, ethical and subversive' traditions (DeVerteuil, 2017, 1520). In some policy areas, newer movements have called on larger charities to end collaborative relationships with government, and urged them to take a more critical stance towards austerity and neoliberal reforms (Moth and Lavalette, 2019, 131). In line with some of the interviewees' reflections, many of these emerging civil-society movements have sought to explicitly distinguish their spaces and practices from the 'consensual stances and technocratic practices' adopted by many voluntary organisations (Ishkanian and Ali, 2018, 14). In many ways, just as in the rest of the UK, this research seems to be capturing debates and discussions on the future of the VCS, but these debates are at an embryonic stage.

SIX

Conclusion

The previous chapters have captured how NI's VCS has had a privileged role in the governance of the region as a result of direct-rule efforts to fill the political vacuum and build some kind of connection with the governed, and as a consequence of devolved administrations' belief that a 'vibrant and extensive' VCS would bring certain advantages. Its position was secured by the development of close relationships between VCS elites, civil servants and funding bodies, a huge flow of resources into its coffers and a narrative that celebrated the sector as the 'glue holding society together'. The VCS came to see itself as a representative forum, with a myriad of funded organisations claiming to speak on behalf of a range of groups and communities. It has been placed at the heart of efforts to refresh civil society–government relations and it has been hailed as the source of innovative solutions to complex problems. The VCS and government promoted the idea that the sector is a wealth of knowledge, and both made the claim that the sector could build trust within and between communities and provide a voice for marginalised communities. To shore up its vacuum-filling role, the VCS has been the beneficiary of extraordinary funding packages, and a service-delivery sector has run alongside a well-funded peace industry. The VCS became central to the delivery of strategies that promised to tackle community divisions, close the gap between the most deprived neighbourhoods and the rest of society, and deliver marginalised communities their share of the 'peace dividend'.

At the grassroots, the VCS can be the locus for the development of a sense of belonging in communities, and networked relationships allow the sector to draw resources into some of the most deprived and conflict-torn communities. In some areas, the VCS has been a site for stimulating economic development, better community relations, employment, training and education opportunities, and without romanticising such initiatives, the research literature is beginning to capture the ways in which they may offer 'alternatives to sectarian, neoliberal or state hegemonies' (Murtagh, 2018, 456). In a similar vein, we need to bear in mind that research that focuses on the reflections of a segment of VCS professionals, and the intricacies of the politics and economics of voluntary action and partnership, is just one part of a wider story that needs to include the voices of the beneficiaries of VCS organisations (Butler et al, 2019). The VCS allows for the development of partnership arrangements with other actors, some in the sector take risks by reaching out to communities across the divide, and the partnerships that are formed can have an impact on complex issues that neither the sector nor government agencies could deal with alone. There is no doubt that some sector groups provide much-needed services to some of the most deprived and marginalised individuals and communities in Northern Irish society (such as asylum seekers, migrants, the long-term unemployed and ex-prisoners and combatants). At times, only VCS groups may be trustworthy enough for marginalised groups to reach out to and seek help from, and they can be a link between marginalised or deprived communities and decision makers. The VCS often takes on unfashionable causes, and by building vertical partnerships and relationships, it is one of the few mechanisms whereby the voice of the voiceless is heard (if not necessarily listened to) in the corridors of power. In other words, the sector helps fill a vacuum in service delivery by providing services for hard-to-reach groups and communities, as well as filling a vacuum in the representation and articulation of diverse needs and interests. Undoubtedly, the COVID-19 pandemic will also have reaffirmed the sector's role in providing essential services to some of the most vulnerable members of society (Harris, 2020).

Over the past few decades, discourses in NI about the VCS and its relationship with government have been peppered with the third-wayist language of networks, linkage, interconnectedness, efficiency, diversity, interdependencies and social capital. As Chapter Three showed, connectionist ideas have been internalised by some actors, with many interviewees drawing on the language of networks, partnership building and social capital. NI is, then, in microcosm, an example of the general trend in democratic societies to develop and mobilise cooperative dispositions, networks and social capital to deliver government objectives. Reflecting the participation and partnership 'turns' in policy discourses, multi-level and multi-actor strategies, forums and networks became embedded within the institutional landscape of NI. Connections came to be seen as an important resource by the VCS and government alike, and their accumulation a valued end goal in and of itself. This research began with the premise that the study of networks, partnerships and relationship building is important, particularly in this policy environment. However, as Chapter Three pointed out, discourses in NI have used very structural notions of social capital and partnership, and with this conflation of network structures and social capital, a celebrated mass of connectivity is in itself seen as social capital. However, from decontextualised headcounts of organisations and their linkages, we learn very little about why, and in whose interests, any particular network or relationship came into existence. We know nothing of the nature and quality of the interactions in a partnership or network, or how it was capable of producing a particular outcome. This research has therefore sought to 'grasp the nature, quality and purpose of connections and the power relations they embody' (Davies, 2011a, 5).

In Chapter Four we viewed this investment in partnership, and the discourses of partnership, through an alternative lens, problematising some of the claims made in Chapter Three. Here we find that many interviewees are sceptical about the motivations within the VCS to engage in partnership or formal and informal horizontal networks. We capture a sense that such cooperation is largely funding led and inspired by top-down edicts, and a sense that the sector has unthinkingly rode waves of funding that mandated partnership practices. The role of EU peace funding, although never a direct focus of this study, certainly looms large in the background in this respect. With massive expenditure over 25 years, a significant portion of which has been invested in VCS projects and capacity building, there is hardly a corner of Northern Irish civil society left untouched by EU funding. As we have seen in other countries in receipt of substantial investment in their civil societies, such funding tends to have significant influence on the development of the VCS, shaping the preferences, priorities and objectives of organisations in its own image (Carothers, 1997; Fagan, 2011; Ketola, 2013; Kuzmanovic, 2013; Zihnioglu, 2013; Wunsch, 2018), and instrumentalising the VCS's role in the service of broad, programme-level goals.

As the previous chapters illustrated, in NI, all the main parties in the devolved administration have actively courted and embraced the VCS, and civil servants interviewed for this research also emphasised the 'special relationship' that exists between the VCS and government. This is hardly surprising in the context of NI's 'double transition' to both peace and neoliberalism (McCabe, 2013, 4). Support for the sector, and 'community' more generally, has been part of the neoliberal strategy to promote communities as a compensatory mechanism for the inadequacies of the market (Jessop, 2002, 455) and the underfunding of the welfare state (Raco, 2003, 243; Raco, 2005, 33), and there is no reason why NI should escape such trends. Executive parties celebrate their efforts to 're-balance the economy' away from the public sector, with all the casualisation, non-unionisation, lower wages and increased job insecurity that this entails. As was captured in the reflections of some interviewees, the policies behind the neoliberal assault on the state and universal welfare has been seen as an 'opportunity' for the VCS. Organisations in NI's VCS have, like their counterparts in other regions, been stuck in a 'race to the bottom', with government offering them less and less and asking them to achieve more and more, but within strict parameters set by government (Acheson, 2013, 10). This democratically unaccountable and non-universal sector (see NCIA, 2015) must deal with particular groups, clients and 'customers' in isolation and as we have seen, fragmented and siloed responses to difficult challenges is a key theme running through the interviews. Competition for a 'partnership' with government has reinforced vertical relationships rather than nurturing horizontal ones, and organisations, communities, identities and groups compete against each other for resources.

As illustrated in Chapters Three, Four and Five, there seems to be two contradictory ideological projects at work in the region, one built on rolling out collaborative norms and values and one premised on embedding and normalising competitive norms and values in more areas of society. But as Hall (2011, 713) argues, 'an ideology is always contradictory' and 'works best by suturing together contradictory lines of argument'. In NI, during the New Labour boom period for the VCS, third-wayism stitched together the idea of a VCS that is enterprising (that is, internally competitive) with the idea that the sector acts as the 'glue that holds society together'. The existence of a generous and unsustainable pot of funding seems to have masked the fact that the inculcation of competitive norms was central to the third-way variant of 'mongrel neoliberalism' (Peck, 2013, 135) taking shape in NI, for as one respondent puts it, 'when we are all being funded everyone is happy to work with everybody'. As there was enough money to go around during the post-peace process funding boom, organisational competition was hidden behind an opaque babble of discourses about joined-up working and building social capital.

That funding boom is now over, and NI has joined the rest of the UK in a process of government–VCS decoupling, rationalising and centralising tendencies in government, instrumental government–VCS relationships, and a suggestion in some quarters that volunteers can replace paid staff. During the heady days of the funding boom, the sector could make big claims about its capacity to cooperate with others in the delivery of innovative solutions to poverty and spatial deprivation, even if those 'solutions' have failed spectacularly in addressing the problems they were apparently designed to be dealing with. The VCS could also make big claims about a cooperative ethos and shared values, yet organisational survival and empire building are now perhaps some of the few 'shared commitments' left. There was an inevitability to this, for in the long term there was no reason why the sector would be spared the competition, monopolisation, predation, centralisation, exploitation and the 'commodification and commercialization of everything' (Harvey, 2002, 107; see also Harvey, 2005; Harvey, 2012), which comes with neoliberalism. The trend towards monopolisation and centralisation is clear in the interviews, with larger well-placed and well-resourced organisations more able to bid for bigger and bigger contracts. The funding environment has now enrolled so many actors into competitive relations that it is difficult to sustain long-term horizontal linkages, even between organisations that have relatively good relationships.

There is often a sense in the interviews that VCS workers see the competition between communities and organisations as an unfortunate by-product of the funding system, and they suggest that government funding and tendering made this competition happen. However, it is worth bearing in mind that the third way sought to inculcate neoliberal rationalities: a competitive ethos and entrepreneurialism coupled with a cooperative and non-adversarial disposition. Interviewees bemoan 'empire building', and how, with organisations 'trampling over the top' of others, cooperative relations are difficult to sustain. However, neoliberalism, including neoliberalism in its third-way guise, celebrates accumulation. Interviewees suggest that the difficulty is that some organisations measure their success by the amount of money they have raised, but under neoliberalism, this is the only measure that counts.

A clear theme emerging from the interviews is that one of the supposed roles of the VCS is linking disadvantaged communities with those who hold power and resources, and government actions would suggest that it has recognised the VCS as the legitimate voice of different groups and communities. As the interviewees suggest, politicians and the departments actively seek out the help and knowledge of the sector. The policy literature seems to suggest that networks and partnerships would come about and be sustained by a recognition on the part of elites (that is, government) that they need the creativity, knowledge and innovativeness of less powerful groups (that is, the VCS) to deal with problems. This is a view reflected in the language of some of the VCS workers when they talk about the sector's capacity to tell government and experts 'what works'. Government has committed resources for the creation and maintenance of structures that allow for vertical government–VCS networking. These kinds of forums range from high-level interactions between sectoral elites and departments, a network of forums and partnerships that bring statutory agencies and VCS groups together, infrastructural spaces in the sector and informal, 'under-the-radar' linkages. The VCS has reciprocated, spending time and effort on engaging with government departments and politicians.

However, like many areas that have been the 'beneficiaries' of top-down efforts to grow civil society, NI has seen the emergence of a bureaucracy that is staffed by a 'project class' (Kovách and Kučerová, 2006, 16). In terms of social composition, status and background, this project class is internally differentiated, with bureaucratic and service-delivery managers and administrators sitting alongside a diverse range of 'community-sector' actors. Emerging out of this project class is a voluntary-sector bureaucracy that is part of an elite-recognised governance 'fraternity'. In terms of social, economic and symbolic capital, the credentialed VCS administrators have little sense of being junior partners when they meet with politicians and officials in collaborative spaces. Alongside the other social and political processes that have shaped the VCS (see Chapter Five), it is easy to see why any disagreement takes places within tightly constrained parameters, and why the 'solutions' proposed are unthreatening to middle-class sensibilities. As we have seen, challenge descends to the level of policy implementation minutiae and technocratic tweaks to overarching policy narratives. In other words, only those who have accepted the overarching policy direction, the 'hegemonic storyline' (Torfing, 2007, 126) can realistically be included in government-sponsored spaces, not least because dissent is often constructed as taboo within such partnerships (Davies, 2009, 84).

Perhaps what this research has most succinctly captured is a sense of 'non-belonging' (Touraine, 1995, 274, in Davies, 2011a, 141) in the VCS as currently constituted, and a concern about where the 'heart and soul' of the sector now lies. For some of the interviewees, there does seem to be a 'them' and an 'us': a very unclear and undefined 'non-incorporated' civil society of 'us', and a 'them' of government and elite-recognised sectoral 'experts' and administrators. As a number of interviewees suggest, the clear dividing line here may be one of class. For those who wish to put class at the centre of their analysis and arguments, there seems to be a creeping realisation that vertical connections are good for the VCS if the existence of the sector is an end in itself, but that the connections become useless or even harmful if the purpose of the VCS is to change society and fight against austerity. With a drying up of funding, with a realisation that working-class areas have been 'sold a pup' in terms of shared ownership of decision making, and with little evidence of a peace dividend, there is waning enthusiasm for the partnership narrative in some quarters of the sector. Perhaps sections of the VCS need to capture this sense of non-belonging and see it as an asset. As hinted at by some interviewees, the time may now be ripe for organisations to begin to more fully consider the implications of a move away from partnership-based community development, and a move towards community organising that is grounded in a rediscovery of 'creative chaos'.

Notes

Chapter One

[1] Note that, as Harris (2005) argues, perceptions of who was eligible for inclusion varied enormously at different times and in different contexts.

[2] See https://www.charitycommissionni.org.uk/about-us/about-the-charity-commission/our-status/

[3] See https://www.charitycommissionni.org.uk/manage-your-charity/register-your-charity/combined-list-and-expression-of-intent-form/#more

Chapter Two

[1] Evidence suggests that the UK already enjoyed healthy levels of volunteering in comparative European terms (see Ketola, 2012).

[2] As Kilmurry (2017, 275) suggests, in discussions around disarmament, demobilisation and reintegration and the funding of ex-prisoner groups, 'paramilitary ex-combatants and prisoners were quick to compare the hefty financial arrangements put in place to cover the severance pay and compensation for security personnel and prison officers, with the lack of any mainstream provision for reintegration and resettlement'.

Chapter Three

[1] Vertical networks are made up of sectoral organisations and agencies that are external to the VCS, such as government and funders. The notion of 'horizontal networks' captures the web of intra-sectoral relationships and partnerships, and the relationships that span different communities.

[2] For example, in some areas CDOs established 'mobile phone networks' to help address sporadic interface tensions and facilitate communication among the CDWs.

[3] It is important to note that this notion of CDWs acting as 'community representatives' would be seen as highly problematic for some other community-sector interviewees. Some CDWs argue that there needs to be greater awareness that, while an organisation may appear to be embedded within a particular community, that doesn't mean it is necessarily connected to that community in any meaningful way. In some cases, interviewees argue, an organisation may only be connected to a proportion of the community, and therefore it shouldn't claim to speak on behalf of the wider community. As one interviewee suggests, their organisation has a valid role in the community, but 'at any given time there are many people out there who do not use us, may not support us, may actively oppose us, so we do not claim to speak on behalf of this community'.

[4] The deal for restoring the institutions, 'New Decade, New Approach', was announced by the British and Irish Governments on 9 January 2020, and was endorsed by the region's political parties a few days later (see Hayward et al, 2020).

[5] Special advisors.

References

Acheson, N. (1995) A partnership of dilemmas and contradictions: Unresolved issues in government–voluntary sector relations, in N. Acheson and A. Williamson (eds) *Voluntary Action and Social Policy in Northern Ireland*, Aldershot: Ashgate Publishing, pp 33–45.

Acheson, N. (2009) Northern Ireland and the independence of the voluntary sector, in M. Smerdon (ed) *The First Principle of Voluntary Action*, London: Baring Foundation, pp 67–82.

Acheson, N. (2010) Welfare state reform, compacts and restructuring relations between the state and the voluntary sector: Reflections on Northern Ireland experience, *Voluntary Sector Review*, 1(2), 175–92.

Acheson, N. (2013) *Independence as a Principle of Voluntary Action: Developing a New Story about Who We Are: The Challenge for Voluntary Action in Northern Ireland*, Belfast: Building Change Trust.

Acheson, N. (2014) Change and the practices of actors in civil society: Towards an interpretivist exploration of agency in third sector scholarship, *Voluntary Sector Review*, 5(3), 293–312.

Acheson, N. and Milofsky, C. (2008) Peace building and participation in Northern Ireland: Local social movements and the policy process since the 'Good Friday' Agreement, *Ethnopolitics*, 7(1), 63–80.

Acheson, N. and Williamson, A. (eds) (1995) *Voluntary Action and Social Policy in Northern Ireland*, Aldershot: Avebury Press.

Acheson, N., Harvey, B., Kearney, J. and Williamson, A. (2004) *Two Paths, One Purpose: Voluntary Action in Ireland, North and South*, Dublin: Institute for Public Administration.

Acheson, N., Harvey, B. and Williamson, A. (2005) State welfare and the development of voluntary action: The case of Ireland, north and south, *Voluntas*, 16(2), 181–202.

Acheson, N., Cairns, E., Stringer, M. and Williamson, A. (2006) *Voluntary Action and Community Relations in Northern Ireland*, Coleraine: Centre for Voluntary Action Studies.

Acheson, N., Milofsky, C. and Stringer, M. (2011) Understanding the role of non-aligned civil society in peacebuilding in Northern Ireland: Towards a fresh approach, in M. Power (ed) *Building Peace in Northern Ireland*, Liverpool: Liverpool University Press, pp 18–36.

Adshead, M. and Tonge, J. (2009) *Politics in Ireland*, London: Palgrave Macmillan.

Aiken, M. and Harris, M. (2017) The 'hollowing out' of smaller third sector organisations?, *Voluntary Sector Review*, 8(3), 333–42.

Aiken, M. and Taylor, M. (2019) Civic action and volunteering: The changing space for popular engagement in England, *Voluntas*, 30(1), 15–28.

Alcock, P. (2010) A strategic unity: Defining the third sector in the UK, *Voluntary Sector Review*, 1(1), 5–24.

Alcock, P. (2016a) The history of third sector service delivery in the UK, in J. Rees and D. Mullins (eds) *The Third Sector Delivering Public Services*, Bristol: Policy Press, pp 21–40.

Alcock, P. (2016b) From partnership to the Big Society: The third sector policy regime in the UK, *Nonprofit Policy Forum*, 7(2), 95–116.

Alcock, P. and Scott, D. (2002) Partnerships with the voluntary sector: Can compacts work?, in C. Glendinning, M. Powell and K. Rummery (eds) *Partnerships, New Labour and the Governance of Welfare*, Bristol: Policy Press, pp 113–30.

Alcock, P. and Kendall, J. (2010) Constituting the third sector: Processes of decontestation and contention under the UK Labour governments in England, *Third Sector Research Centre Working Paper 42*, Birmingham: University of Birmingham.

Atkinson, R. (1999) Discourses of partnership and empowerment in contemporary British urban regeneration, *Urban Studies*, 36(1), 59–72.

Bach, S. (2012) Shrinking the state or the Big Society? Public service employment relations in an era of austerity, *Industrial Relations Journal*, 43(5), 399–415.

Baines, D. and Cunningham, I. (2015) Care work in the context of austerity, *Competition & Change*, 19(3), 183–93.

Baker, S. (2014) Belfast: New battle-lines in a post-conflict city, *New Left Project*, 11 March.

Barry, J. (2019) Class, political economy and loyalist political disaffection: Agonistic politics and the flag protests, *Global Discourse*, 9(3), 457–77.

Birrell, D. (2012a) *Comparing Devolved Governance*, London: Palgrave Macmillan.

Birrell, D. (2012b) Is the Idea that Northern Ireland is over-governed a myth?, *Policy Briefing. Assembly Knowledge Exchange Seminar Series*, Belfast: Stormont Assembly.

Birrell, D. and Williamson, A. (2001) The voluntary–community sector and political development in Northern Ireland, since 1972, *Voluntas*, 12(3), 205–20.

Birrell, D. and Gormley-Heenan, C. (2015) *Multi-Level Governance and Northern Ireland*, London: Palgrave Macmillan.

Blair, T. (1998) Speech at the Royal Agricultural Show, 14 May, Belfast, http://cain.ulst.ac.uk/events/peace/docs/tb14598.htm

Blair, T. (1999) Speech to the National Council for Voluntary Organisations annual conference, 21 January, London.

Blair, T. (2000) Speech to the annual conference of the Women's Institute, 7 June, London.

Body, A. and Kendall, J. (2020) Expansive opportunity makers but selective opportunity takers? Positional agility and tactical social skill in English third sector social service, *Journal of Civil Society*, 16(1), 15–34.

Boland, P. (2014) The relationship between spatial planning and economic competitiveness: The 'path to economic nirvana' or a 'dangerous obsession'?, *Environment and Planning A*, 46(4), 770–87.

Boland, P., Bronte, J. and Muir, J. (2017) On the waterfront: Neoliberal urbanism and the politics of public benefit, *Cities*, 61, 117–27.

Braniff, M. and Byrne, J. (2014) Circle of friends: Unravelling the networks of peacebuilding in Northern Ireland, *Peacebuilding*, 2(1), 45–63.

Breeze, B. and Mohan, J. (2020) Sceptical yet supportive: Understanding public attitudes to charity, *History & Policy*, 28 April, http://www.historyandpolicy.org/policy-papers/papers/sceptical-yet-supportive-understanding-public-attitudes-to-charity

Brenner, N., Peck, J. and Theodore, N. (2010) After neoliberalization?, *Globalizations*, 7(3), 327–45.

Brown, G. (2006) Remarks by the Rt Hon Gordon Brown MP, Chancellor of the Exchequer, at the HMRC Corporate & Social Responsibility Conference with His Royal Highness, The Prince of Wales, at HM Treasury, 24 October.

Buckingham, H. (2012) Capturing diversity: a typology of third sector organisations, responses to contracting based on empirical evidence from homelessness services, *Journal of Social Policy*, 41(3), 569–89.

Buckingham, H. and Rees, J. (2016) The context for service delivery: third sector, state and market relationships 1997–2015, in J. Rees and D. Mullins (eds) *The Third Sector Delivering Public Services*, Bristol: Policy Press, pp 41–62.

Butler, M., McLaughlin, A., Hayes, D. and Percy, A. (2019) *Supporting Children and Families with Complex Needs: An Exploration of the Risks and Benefits of Voluntary Sector Service Provision as an Alternative to Statutory Services*, Belfast: Queens University Belfast.

Campbell, A., Hughes, J., Hewstone, M. and Cairns, E. (2008) Social capital as a mechanism for building a sustainable society in Northern Ireland, *Community Development Journal*, 45(1), 22–38.

Carmel, E. and Harlock, J. (2008) Instituting the 'third sector' as a governable terrain: partnership, procurement and performance in the UK, *Policy and Politics*, 36(2), 155–71.

Carmichael, P. (2002) The Northern Ireland civil service: Characteristics and trends since 1970, *Public Administration*, 80(1), 23–49.

Carmichael, P. and Knox, C. (2004) Devolution, governance and the peace process, *Terrorism and Political Violence*, 16(3), 593–621.

Carmichael, P. and Knox, C. (2005) The reform of public administration in Northern Ireland: From principles to practice, *Political Studies*, 53(4), 772–92.

Carothers, T. (1997) Democracy assistance: the question of strategy, *Democratization*, 4(3), 109–32.

Chater, D. (2008) Coming in from the cold? The impact of the contract culture on voluntary sector homelessness agencies in England, *Voluntary Sector Working Papers* 10, London: LSE Centre for Civil Society.

Chew, C. and Osborne, S.P. (2009) Exploring strategic positioning in the UK charitable sector: Emerging evidence from charitable organisations that provide public services, *British Journal of Management*, 20(1), 90–105.

Clark, T. (2002) New Labour's big idea: Joined-up government, *Social Policy and Society*, 1(2), 107–17.

Clarke, J., Gerwitz, S. and McLaughlin, E. (2000) Reinventing the welfare state, in J. Clarke, S. Gerwitz and E. McLaughlin (eds) *New Managerialism, New Welfare?*, London: Sage, pp 1–26.

Clayton, J., Donovan, C. and Merchant, J. (2016) Distancing and limited resourcefulness: Third sector service provision under austerity localism in the north east of England, *Urban Studies*, 53(4), 723–40.

Cochrane, A. (1999) Just another failed experiment? The legacy of the Urban Development Corporations, in R. Imire and H. Thomas (eds) *British Urban Policy: An Evaluation of the Urban Development Corporations*, London: Sage, pp 246–58.

Cochrane, F. (2000) Beyond the political elites: A comparative analysis of the roles and impacts of community-based NGOs in conflict resolution activity, *Civil Wars*, 3(2), 1–22.

Conservative Party (2008) *A Stronger Society: Voluntary Action in the 21st Century*, London: Conservative Party

Corbett, S. and Walker, A. (2012) The Big Society: Back to the future, *The Political Quarterly*, 83(3), 487–93.

Corcoran, M.S. (2017) Resilient hearts: Making affective citizens for neoliberal times, *Justice, Power & Resilience*, 1(2), 283–99.

Corcoran, M.S., Williams, K., Prince, K. and Maguire, M. (2018) The penal voluntary sector in England and Wales: Adaptation to unsettlement and austerity, *The Political Quarterly*, 89(2), 187–96

Corcoran, M.S., Maguire, M. and Williams, K. (2019) Alice in wonderland: Voluntary sector organisations' experiences of transforming rehabilitation, *Probation Journal*, 66(1), 96–112.

Coule, T.M. and Bennett, E. (2018) State–voluntary relations in contemporary welfare systems: New politics or voluntary action as usual?, *Nonprofit and Voluntary Sector Quarterly*, 47(suppl. 4), 139S–158S.

Coulter, C. (2014) Under which constitutional arrangement would you still prefer to be unemployed? Neoliberalism, the peace process, and the politics of class in Northern Ireland, *Studies in Conflict & Terrorism*, 37(9), 763–76.

Coulter, C. (2019) Northern Ireland's elusive peace dividend: Neoliberalism, austerity and the politics of class, *Capital & Class*, 43(1), 123–38.

Couto, R.A. (2001) The third sector and civil society: The case of the 'YES' campaign in Northern Ireland, *Voluntas*, 12(3), 221–38.

Coyles, D. (2013) Reflections on Titanic Quarter: The cultural and material legacy of an historic Belfast brand, *The Journal of Architecture*, 18(3), 331–63.

Crawford, A. (2001) Joined-up but fragmented: Contradiction, ambiguity and ambivalence at the heart of New Labour's 'Third Way', in R. Matthews and J. Pitts (eds) *Crime, Disorder and Community Safety: A New Agenda?*, London: Routledge, pp 54–80.

Crowson, N.J. (2011) Introduction: The voluntary sector in 1980s Britain, *Contemporary British History*, 25(4), 491–8.

CRU (Community Relations Unit) (2005) *A Shared Future: Improving Relations in Northern Ireland: The Policy and Strategic Framework for Good Relations in Northern Ireland*, Belfast: Office of the First Minister and Deputy First Minister.

Cunningham, I. and James, P. (2009) The outsourcing of social care in Britain: What does it mean for voluntary sector workers?, *Work, Employment and Society*, 23(2), 363–75.

Cunningham, I. and Nickson, D. (2011) A gathering storm: Re-tendering and the voluntary sector workforce, *International Journal of Public Sector Management*, 24(7), 662–72.

Dagdeviren, H., Donoghue, M. and Wearmouth, A. (2019) When rhetoric does not translate to reality: Hardship, empowerment and the third sector in austerity localism, *The Sociological Review*, 67(1), 143–60.

Davies, J.S. (2004) Conjuncture or disjuncture? An institutionalist analysis of local regeneration partnerships in the UK, *International Journal of Urban and Regional Research*, 28(3), 570–85.

Davies, J.S. (2005) Local governance and the dialectics of hierarchy, market and network, *I*, 26(3–4), 311–33.

Davies, J.S. (2008) Double-devolution or double-dealing? The local government white paper and the Lyons Review, *Local Government Studies*, 34(1), 3–22.

Davies, J.S. (2009) The limits of joined-up government: Towards a political analysis, *Public Administration*, 87(1), 80–96.

Davies, J.S. (2010) Back to the future: Marxism and urban politics, in J.S. Davies and D.L. Imbroscio (eds) *Critical Urban Studies: New Directions*, New York: SUNY Press, pp 73–88.

Davies, J.S. (2011a) *Challenging Governance Theory: From Networks to Hegemony*, Bristol: Policy Press.

Davies, J.S. (2011b) The limits of post-traditional public administration: Towards a Gramscian perspective, *Critical Policy Studies*, 5(1), 47–62.

Davies, J.S. (2012a) Network governance theory: A Gramscian critique, *Environment and Planning A*, 4(11), 2687–704.

Davies, J.S. (2012b) Active citizenship: Navigating the conservative heartlands of the New Labour project, *Policy & Politics* 40(1), 3–19.

Davies, J.S. and Pill, M. (2012) Empowerment or abandonment? Prospects for neighbourhood revitalization under the Big Society, *Public Money & Management*, 32(3), 193–200.

Deakin, N. (2001) Public policy, social policy and voluntary organisations, in M. Harris and C. Rochester (eds) *Voluntary Organisations and Social Policy in Britain*, London: Palgrave, pp 21–36.

DeVerteuil, G. (2017) Post-welfare city at the margins: Immigrant precarity and the mediating third sector in London, *Urban Geography*, 38(10), 1517–33.

DfC (Department for Communities) (2017) *A Consultation Paper on Proposals for the Provision of Strategic Support to the Voluntary and Community Sector in Northern Ireland 2017–2021*, https://www.communities-ni.gov.uk/consultations/consultation-proposals-provision-strategic-supportvoluntary-and-community-sector-northern-ireland

DHSS (Department of Health and Social Services) (1993) *Strategy for Support of the Voluntary Sector and for Community Development*, Belfast: DHSS

Dixon, P. (1997) Paths to peace in Northern Ireland (II): The peace processes 1973–74 and 1994–96, *Democratization*, 4(3), 1–25.

Dixon, P. (2001) British policy towards Northern Ireland 1969–2000: Continuity, tactical adjustment and consistent 'inconsistencies', *The British Journal of Politics and International Relations*, 3(3), 340–68.

Dixon, P. (2009) 'Hearts and minds'? British counter-insurgency strategy in Northern Ireland, *Journal of Strategic Studies*, 32(3), 445–74.

DSD (Department for Social Development) (2003) *Partners for Change: A Government Strategy for the Support of Voluntary and Community Organizations*, Belfast: Department for Social Development.

DSD (Department for Social Development) (2006) *Toolkit to Measure the Added Value of Voluntary and Community Based Activity*, Belfast: Department of Social Development.

DSD (Department for Social Development) (2011) *Concordat between the Voluntary and Community Sector and the Northern Ireland Government*, Belfast: Department for Social Development.

Dunn, A. (2000) Shoots among the grassroots: Political activity and the independence of the voluntary sector, in A. Dunn (ed) *The Voluntary Sector, the State and the Law*, Oxford: Hart Publishing, pp 143–160.

Dunn, A. (2006) To foster or to temper? Regulating the political activities of the voluntary and community sector, *Legal Studies*, 26(4), 500–23.

Edwards, M. (2009) *Civil Society*, Cambridge: Polity Press.

Eikenberry, A.M. (2009) Refusing the market: A democratic discourse for voluntary and nonprofit organizations, *Nonprofit and Voluntary Sector Quarterly*, 38(4), 582–96.

Egdell, V. and Dutton, M. (2017) Third sector independence: Relations with the state in an age of austerity, *Voluntary Sector Review* 8(1), 25–40.

Enjolras, E., Salomon, L.M., Sivesind, K.H. and Zimmer, A. (eds) (2018) *Third Sector as a Renewable Resource for Europe*, Basingstoke: Palgrave Macmillan.

Fagan, A. (2011) EU assistance for civil society in Kosovo: a step too far for democracy promotion?, *Democratization*, 18(3), 707–30.

Fairclough, N. (2000) *New Labour, New Language*, London: Routledge.

Fenton, S. (2018) *The Good Friday Agreement*, London: Biteback Publishing.

Ferguson, N. and Halliday, D. (2020) Collective memory and the legacy of the Troubles: Territoriality, identity and victimhood in Northern Ireland, in J.R. Vollhardt (ed) *The Social Psychology of Collective Victimhood*, Oxford: Oxford University Press, pp 56–74.

Field, J. (2003) *Social Capital*, London: Routledge.

Fine, B. (2010) *Theories Of Social Capital: Researchers Behaving Badly*, London: Pluto Press.

Fitzduff, M. (1995) Managing community relations and conflict: voluntary organizations and government and the search for peace, in N. Acheson and A. Williamson (eds) *Voluntary Action and Social Policy in Northern Ireland*, Aldershot: Avebury, pp 63–81.

Foley, M.W. and Edwards, B. (1998) Beyond Tocqueville: Civil society and social capital in comparative perspective, *American Behavioral Scientist*, 42(1), 5–20.

Foley, P. and Martin, S. (2000) A new deal for the community? Public participation in regeneration and local service delivery, *Policy and Politics*, 28(4), 479–91.

Fordham, G., Hutchinson, J. and Foley, P. (1999) Strategic approaches to local regeneration: The single regeneration budget challenge fund, *Regional Studies*, 33(2), 131–41.

Fyfe, N.R. (2005) Making space for 'neo-communitarianism'? The third sector, state and civil society in the UK, *Antipode*, 37(3), 536–57.

Gilchrist, V.J. (1992) Key informant interviews, in B.F. Crabtree and W.L. Miller (eds) *Doing Qualitative Research*, London: Sage, pp 70–89.

Goldstraw, K. (2018) Using creativity to envision a good society, *Local Economy*, 33(6), 615–35.

Granovetter, M.S. (1973) The strength of weak ties, *American Journal of Sociology*, 78(6), 1360–80.

Gray, A.M. and Birrell, D. (2011) Coalition government in Northern Ireland: Social policy and the lowest common denominator thesis, *Social Policy & Society*, 11(1), 15–25.

Greer, J. (2001) Whither partnership governance in Northern Ireland?, *Environment and Planning C: Government and Policy*, 19(5), 751–70.

Griffiths, H. (1972) The Northern Ireland Community Relations Commission, *Journal of Ethnic and Migration Studies*, 1(2), 128–32.

Griffiths, H. (1975) Paramilitary groups and other community action groups in Northern Ireland today, *International Review of Community Development*, 33(4), 189–206.

Guelke, A. (2003) Civil society and the Northern Irish peace process, *Voluntas*, 14(1), 61–78.

Hall, S. (2011) The neo-liberal revolution, *Cultural Studies*, 25(6), 705–28.

Halpern, D. (2005) *Social Capital*, Bristol: Policy Press.

Hancock, L.E. (2019) Deliberative peacebuilding: Agency and development in post-conflict practice, *Peacebuilding*, 8(2), 139–58.

Harris, B. (2010) Voluntary action and the state in historical perspective, *Voluntary Sector Review*, 1(1), 25–40.

Harris, J. (2005) *Civil Society in British History: Ideas, Identities, Institutions*, Oxford: Oxford University Press.

Harris, M. (2020) Familiar patterns and new initiatives: UK civil society and government initial responses to the Covid-19 crisis, *Nonprofit Policy Forum*, 12(1), 25–44.

Harris, M., Rochester, C. and Halfpenny, P. (2001) Voluntary organisations and social policy: Twenty years of change, in M. Harris and C. Rochester (eds) *Voluntary Organisations and Social Policy in Britain*, London: Palgrave, pp 1–20.

Harvey, D. (2002) The art of rent: Globalization, monopoly and the commodification of culture, *Socialist Register*, 38(2), 93–110.

Harvey, D. (2005) *A Brief History of Neoliberalism*, Oxford: Oxford University Press.

Harvey, D. (2006) Neoliberalism as creative destruction, *Geografiska Annaler: Series B, Human Geography*, 88(2), 145–58.

Harvey, D. (2007a) *A Brief History of Neoliberalism,* Oxford: Oxford University Press.

Harvey, D. (2007b) Neoliberalism as creative destruction, *The Annals of the American Academy of Political and Social Science*, 610(1), 21–44.

Harvey, D. (2012) *Rebel Cities: From the Right to the City to the Urban Revolution*, London, New York: Verso.

Hastings, A. (2003) Strategic, multi-level neighbourhood regeneration: An outward looking approach at last?, in R. Imrie and M. Raco (eds) *Urban Renaissance? New Labour, Community and Urban Policy,* Bristol: Policy Press, pp 85–100.

Haugh, H. and Kitson, M. (2007) The third way and the third sector: New Labour's economic policy and the social economy, *Cambridge Journal of Economics*, 31(6), 973–94.

Hay, C. (1999) *The Political Economy of New Labour: Labouring Under False Pretences?*, Manchester: Manchester University Press.

Hayward, K., Phinnemore, D. and Komarova, M. (2020) *Anticipating and Meeting New Multilevel Governance Challenges in Northern Ireland after Brexit*, London: Economic and Social Research Council.

Hearty, K. (2018) Discourses of political policing in post-Patten Northern Ireland, *Critical Criminology*, 26(1), 129–43.

Heenan, D. and Birrell, D. (2011) *Social Work in Northern Ireland, Conflict and Change*, Bristol: Policy Press.

Hemmings, M. (2017) The constraints on voluntary sector voice in a period of continued austerity, *Voluntary Sector Review*, 8(1), 41–66.

Hendriks, F. and Tops, P. (2005) Everyday fixers as local heroes: a case study of vital interaction in urban governance, *Local Government Studies*, 31(4), 475–90.

Herman, A. and Yarwood, R. (2015) From warfare to welfare: Veterans, military charities and the blurred spatiality of post-service welfare in the United Kingdom, *Environment and Planning A*, 47(12),: 2628–44.

Heron, E. and Dwyer, P. (1999) Doing the right thing: Labour's attempt to forge a new welfare deal between the individual and the state, *Social Policy & Administration*, 33(1), 91–104.

Hesmondhalgh, D., Nisbett, M., Oakley, K. and Lee, D. (2015) Were New Labour's cultural policies neo-liberal?, *International Journal of Cultural Policy*, 21(1), 97–114.

Hillyard, P., Rolston, W. and Tomlinson, M. (2005) *Poverty and Conflict: The International Evidence*, Dublin: Combat Poverty Agency/Institute of Public Administration.

Hodgett, S. (2008) Sen, culture and expanding participatory capabilities in Northern Ireland, *Journal of Human Development*, 9(2), 165–83.

Hodgett, S. and Johnson, D. (2001) Troubles, partnerships and possibilities: A study of the Making Belfast Work development initiative in Northern Ireland, *Public Administration and Development*, 21(4), 321–32.

Hodgson, L. (2004) Manufactured civil society: Counting the cost, *Critical Social Policy*, 24(2), 139–64.

Hoggett, P. (1997) Contested communities, in P. Hogget (ed) *Contested Communities*, Bristol: Policy Press, pp 3–16.

Holland, C. and Rabrenovic, G. (2018) Masculinities in transition? Exclusion, ethnosocial power, and contradictions in excombatant community-based peacebuilding in Northern Ireland, *Men and Masculinities*, 21(5), 729–55.

Horgan, G. (2006) Devolution, direct rule and neo-liberal reconstruction in Northern Ireland, *Critical Social Policy,* 26(12),: 656–66.

Horgan, G. and Gray, A.M. (2012) Devolution in Northern Ireland: A lost opportunity?, *Critical Social Policy* 32(3), 467–78.

Hughes, C. (2015) *Networks, Social Capital and the Voluntary and Community Sector in Northern Ireland.* Unpublished PhD thesis, Queen's University Belfast.

Hughes, C. (2019) Resisting or enabling? The roll-out of neoliberal values through the voluntary and community sector in Northern Ireland, *Critical Policy Studies*, 13(1), 61–80.

Hughes, J. and Carmichael, P. (1998) Community relations in Northern Ireland: Attitudes to contact and integration, in G. Robinson, A.M. Gray and D. Heenan (eds) *Social Attitudes in Northern Ireland: The Seventh Report*, Aldershot: Ashgate, pp 1–19.

Hughes, J., Donnelly, C., Leitch, R. and Burns, S. (2016) Caught in the conundrum: Neoliberalism and education in post-conflict Northern Ireland – exploring shared education, *Policy Futures in Education*, 14(8), 1091–1100.

Imrie, R. and Raco, M. (eds) (2003) *Urban Renaissance: New Labour, Community and Urban Policy*, Bristol: Policy Press.

Inclusive Boards (2018) Charities: Inclusive Governance, London: Inclusive Boards.

Ishkanian, A. and Szreter, S. (eds) (2012) *The Big Society Debate: A New Agenda for Social Welfare?*, Cheltenham: Edward Elgar.

Ishkanian, A. and Irum, S.A. (2018) From consensus to dissensus: The politics of anti-austerity activism in London and its relationship to voluntary organizations, *Journal of Civil Society*, 14(1), 1–19, doi: 10.1080/17448689.2017.1389843

Jessop, B. (2002) Liberalism, neoliberalism and urban governance: A state-theoretical perspective, in N. Brenner and N. Theodore (eds) *Spaces of Neoliberalism: Urban Restructuring in North America and Western Europe*, Oxford: Blackwell, pp 105–25.

Jessop, B. (2003) From Thatcherism to New Labour: Neo-liberalism, workfarism, and labour market regulation, in H. Overbeek (ed) *The Political Economy of European Employment: European Integration and the Transnationalization of the (Un)Employment Question*, London: Routledge, pp 137–153.

Jessop, B. (2007) New Labour or the normalization of neo-liberalism?, *British Politics*, 2(3), 282–8.

Jessop, B. (2015) Margaret Thatcher and Thatcherism: Dead but not buried, *British Politics*, 10(1), 16–30.

Kaviraj, S. and Khilnani, S. (eds) (2001) *Civil Society: History and Possibilities*, Cambridge: Cambridge University Press

Kearney, J. (1995) The development of government policy and its strategy toward the voluntary and community sectors, in N. Acheson and A. Williamson (eds) *Voluntary Action and Social Policy in Northern Ireland*, Aldershot: Ashgate, pp 11–32.

Kearney, J. and Williamson, A. (2001) *The Voluntary and Community Sector in Northern Ireland: Developments Since 1995/6*, London: National Council for Voluntary Organisations.

Kearns, A. (1995) Active citizenship and local governance: Political and geographical dimensions, *Political Geography*, 14(2), 155–75.

Kearns, A. (2003) Social capital, regeneration and urban policy, in R. Imrie and M. Raco (eds) *Urban Renaissance? New Labour, Community and Urban Policy*, Bristol: Policy Press, pp 37–60.

Kelly, G. (2012) Prioritising change: five-year reconciliation imperatives for Northern Ireland, *Shared Space: A Research Journal on Peace, Conflict and Community Relations in Northern Ireland*, 12, 55–71.

Kendall, J. (2000) The mainstreaming of the third sector into public policy in England in the late 1990s: Whys and wherefores, *Policy & Politics*, 28(4), 541–62.

Kendall, J. (ed) (2009) *Handbook of Third Sector Policy in Europe: Multilevel Processes and Organised Civil Society*, Cheltenham: Edward Elgar.

Kendall, J. and Knapp, M. (1995) A loose and baggy monster, in J. Davis Smith, C. Rochester and R. Hedley (eds) *An Introduction to the Voluntary Sector*, London: Routledge, pp 66–95.

Kendall, J., Mohan J., Brookes, N. and Yoon, Y. (2018) The English Voluntary sector: How volunteering and policy climate perceptions matter, *Journal of Social Policy*, 47(4), 759–82.

Ketola, M. (2012) European perspectives on the Big Society agenda, in A. Ishkanian and S. Szreter (eds) *The Big Society Debate: A New Agenda for Social Welfare*, Cheltenham: Edward Elgar, pp 157–168.

Ketola, M. (2013) *Europeanization and Civil Society: Turkish NGOs as Agents of Change?*, Basingstoke: Palgrave Macmillan.

Ketola, M. and Hughes, C. (2016) *Changing Narratives, Changing Relationships: A New Environment For VCSE Action?*, Belfast: Building Change Trust.

Ketola, M. and Hughes, C. (2018) Changing narratives, changing relationships: A new environment for voluntary action?, *Voluntary Sector Review*, 9(2), 197–214.

Kilmurray, A. (2017) *Community Action in a Contested Society: The Story of Northern Ireland*, Oxford: Peter Lang.

Kisby, B. (2010) The Big Society: Power to the people?, *The Political Quarterly*, 81(4), 484–91.

Knox, C. (2014) Northern Ireland: Where is the peace dividend?, *Policy & Politics*, 44(3), 485–503.

Knox, C. and Quirk, P. (2016) *Public Policy, Philanthropy and Peacebuilding in Northern Ireland*, Basingstoke: Palgrave Macmillan.

Kovách, I. and Kučerová, E. (2006) The project class in central Europe: the Czech and Hungarian cases, *Sociologia Ruralis*, 46(1), 3–21.

Kuzmanovic, D. (2012) *Refractions of Civil Society*, Basingstoke and New York: Palgrave Macmillan.

Leggett, W. (2004) Criticism and the future of the third way, in S. Hale, W. Leggett and L. Martell (eds) *The Third Way and Beyond: Criticisms, Futures, Alternatives*, Manchester: Manchester University Press, pp 186–200.

Leonard, M. (2004) Bonding and bridging social capital: Reflection from Belfast, *Sociology*, 38(5), 927–44.

Levitas, R. (2000) Community, utopia and New Labour, *Local Economy*, 15(3), 188–197.

Levitas, R. (2005) *The Inclusive Society? Social Exclusion and New Labour*, Palgrave: Macmillan.

Lewis, J. (1999) Reviewing the relationships between the voluntary sector and the state in Britain in the 1990s, *Voluntas*, 10(3), 255–27.

Lewis, J. (2005) New Labour's approach to the voluntary sector: Independence and the meaning of partnership, *Social Policy and Society*, 4(2), 121–31.

Lindsey, R., Mohan, J., Metcalfe, E. and Bulloch, S. (2018) *Continuity and Change in Voluntary Action: Patterns, Trends and Understandings*, Bristol: Policy Press.

Lister, R. (2003) Investing in the citizen-workers of the future: Transformations in citizenship and the state under New Labour, *Social Policy & Administration*, 37(5), 427–43.

Living Wage Foundation (2018) *Tackling Low Pay In the Charity Sector: An Action Plan*, https://www.livingwage.org.uk/sites/default/files/Action%20Plan%20Report%204.pdf

Lowndes, V. and Sullivan, H. (2004) Like a horse and carriage or a fish on bicycle: How well do local partnerships and public partnerships go together?, *Local Government Studies*, 30(1), 51–73.

Lowndes, V. and Pratchett, L. (2012) Local governance under the Coalition government: Austerity, localism and the 'Big Society', *Local Government Studies*, 38(1), 21–40.

Lowndes, V. and Gardner, A. (2016) Local governance under the Conservatives: super-austerity, devolution and the 'smarter state', *Local Government Studies*, 42(3), 357–75.

MacGinty, R. (2004) Unionist political attitudes after the Belfast agreement, *Irish Political Studies*, 19(1), 87–99.

Macmillan, R. (2010) The third sector delivering public services: An evidence review, *Third Sector Research Centre Working Paper* 20, Birmingham: University of Birmingham.

Macmillan, R. (2012) 'Distinction' in the third sector, *Third Sector Research Centre Working Paper* 89, Birmingham: University of Birmingham.

Macmillan, R. (2013) Decoupling the state and the third sector? The 'Big Society' as a spontaneous order, *Third Sector Research Centre Working Paper 101*, Birmingham: Third Sector Research Centre.

Macmillan, R. (2016) Capacity building for competition: The role of infrastructure in third sector service delivery, in J. Rees and D. Mullins (eds) *The Third Sector Delivering Public Services*, Bristol: Policy Press, pp 107–125.

Maguire, M. (2012) Response 1: Big Society, the voluntary sector and the marketization of criminal justice, *Criminology & Criminal Justice*, 12(5), 483–94.

Marshall, M.N. (1996) Sampling for qualitative research, *Family Practice*, 13(6), 522–5.

May, J., Williams, A., Cloke, P. and Cherry, L. (2019) Welfare convergence, bureaucracy, and moral distancing at the food bank, *Antipode*, 51: 1251–75, doi: 10.1111/anti.12531

McAreavey, R. (2017) *New Immigration Destinations: Migrating to Rural and Peripheral Areas*, New York, NY: Routledge.

McCabe, A., Philllimore, J. and Mayblin, K. (2010) Below the radar activities and organisations in the third sector: a summary review of the literature, *Working Paper*, Birmingham: University of Birmingham.

McCabe, C. (2013) *The Double Transition: The Economic and Political Transition of Peace*, Belfast: Trademark Belfast.

McCall, C. and Williamson, A. (2001) Governance and democracy in Northern Ireland: The role of the voluntary and community sector after the agreement, *Governance: An International Journal of Policy, Administration and Institutions*, 14(3), 363–83.

McCall, C. and O'Dowd, L. (2008) Hanging flower baskets, blowing in the wind? Third-sector groups, cross-border partnerships, and the EU Peace Programs in Ireland, *Nationalism and Ethnic Politics*, 14(1), 29–54.

McEvoy, K. and Shirlow, P. (2009) Re-imagining DDR: Ex-combatants, leadership and moral agency in conflict transformation, *Theoretical Criminology*, 13(1), 31–59.

McKinney, N. (2017) The political crisis in Northern Ireland is bad for charities. Why don't we protest? *Guardian*, 21 November.

McKittrick, D. and McVea, D. (2012) *Making Sense of the Troubles: A History of the Northern Ireland Conflict*, London: Penguin.

McLaughlin, E. (2005) Governance and social policy in Northern Ireland (1999–2002): The devolution years and postscript, in M. Powell, L. Bauld and J. Clarke (eds) *Social Policy Review 17, Analysis and Debate in Social Policy*, Bristol: Policy Press, pp 107–24.

Milbourne, L. (2013) *Voluntary Sector in Transition: Hard Times or New Opportunities?*, Bristol: Policy Press.

Milbourne, L. and Cushman, M. (2013) From the third sector to the Big Society: How changing UK government policies have eroded third sector trust, *Voluntas*, 24(2), 485–508.

Mitchell, C. (2008) The limits of legitimacy: Former Loyalist combatants and peace-building in Northern Ireland, *Irish Political Studies*, 23(1), 1–19.

Morrison, Z. (2005) Cultural justice and addressing social exclusion, in R. Imrie and M. Raco (eds) *Urban Renaissance: New Labour, Community and Urban Policy*, Bristol: Policy Press, pp 139–61.

Morrow, D. (1996) Filling the gap: Policy and pressure under direct rule, in A. Aughey and D. Morrow (eds) *Northern Ireland Politics*, Harlow: Longman, pp 130–41.

Morrow, D. (2017) Reconciliation and after in Northern Ireland: The search for a political order in an ethnically divided society, *Nationalism and Ethnic Politics*, 23(1), 98–117.

Moth, R. and Lavalette, M. (2019) Social policy and welfare movements 'from below': The Social Work Action Network (SWAN) in the UK, in U. Klammer, S. Leiber and S. Leitner (eds) *Social Work and the Making of Social Policy*, Bristol: Policy Press.

Muir, J. (2010) Bridging and linking in a divided society: a social capital case study from Northern Ireland, *Urban Studies*, 48(5), 959–76.

Murtagh, B. (2011) Desegregation and place restructuring in the new Belfast, *Urban Studies*, 48(6), 1119–35.

Murtagh, B. (2018) Contested space, peacebuilding and the post-conflict city, *Parliamentary Affairs*, 71(2): 438–60.

Murtagh, B. and Shirlow, P. (2012) Devolution and the politics of development in Northern Ireland, *Environment and Planning C*, 30(1), 46–61.

Murtagh, B., Graham, B. and Shirlow, P. (2008) Authenticity and stakeholder planning in the segregated city, *Progress in Planning*, 69(2), 41–92.

Nagle, J. (2009) Potemkin village: Neo-liberalism and peace-building in Northern Ireland?, *Ethnopolitics*, 8(2), 173–90.

Nagle, J. (2018) Between conflict and peace: An analysis of the complex consequences of the Good Friday Agreement, *Parliamentary Affairs*, 71(2), 395–416.

NCIA (National Coalition for Independent Action) (2015) *Fight or Fright: Voluntary Services in 2015, NCIA Inquiry into the Future of Voluntary Services*, National Coalition for Independent Action, http://www.independentaction.net/wp-content/uploads/sites/8/2015/02/NCIA-Inquiry-summary-report-final.pdf

Newman, J. (2001) *Modernising Governance: New Labour, Policy and Society*, London: Sage.

Newman, J. (2005) Enter the transformational leader: Network governance and the micro-politics of modernization, *Sociology*, 39(4), 717–34.

NICVA (Northern Ireland Council for Voluntary Action) (2016) *State of the Sector*, Belfast: Northern Ireland Council for Voluntary Action.

Nolan, P. and Wilson, R. (2015) *Dialogue and Engagement: Lessons from the Northern Ireland Civic Forum*, York: Joseph Rowntree Trust.

O'Dowd, L. and Komarova, M. (2013) Three narratives in search of a city, *City*, 17(4), 526–46.

O'Hearn, D. (2008) How has peace changed the Northern Irish economy?, *Ethnopolitics*, 7(1), 101–18.

O'Regan, A. (2001) Contexts and constraints for NPOs: The case of Co-operation Ireland, *Voluntas*, 12(3), 239–56.

Paine, A.E. and Hill, M. (2016) The engagement of volunteers in third sector organisations delivering public services, in J. Rees and D. Mullins (eds) *The Third Sector Delivering Public Services*, Bristol: Policy Press, pp 127–48.

Panel on the Independence of the Voluntary Sector (2014) *Independence Undervalued: The Voluntary Sector in 2014*, London: The Baring Foundation.

Pape, U., Brandsen, T., Pahl, J.B., Pieliński, B., Baturina, D., Brookes, N., Chaves-Ávila, R., Kendall, J., Matančević, J., Petrella, F., Rentzsch, C., Richez-Battesti, N., Savall-Morera, T., Simsa, R. and Zimmer, A. (2020) Changing policy environments in Europe and the resilience of the third sector, *Voluntas*, 31 (2), 238–49.

Peck, J. (2004) Geography and public policy: Constructions of neoliberalism, *Progress in Human Geography*, 28(3), 392–405.

Peck, J. (2010) *Constructions of Neoliberal Reason*, Oxford: Oxford University Press.

Peck, J. (2013) Explaining (with) neoliberalism, *Territory, Politics, Governance*, 1(2), 132–57.

Peck, J. and Theodore, N. (2001) Exporting workfare/importing welfare-to-work: Exploring the politics of third way policy transfer, *Political Geography*, 20, 427–60.

Peck, J. and Tickell, A. (2007) Conceptualising neoliberalism, thinking Thatcherism, in H. Leitner, J. Peck and E.S. Sheppard (eds) *Contesting Neoliberalism: Urban Frontiers*, New York: Guilford Press, pp 26–50.

Peck, J., Theodore, N. and Brenner, N. (2010) Postneoliberalism and its malcontents, *Antipode*, 41(1), 94–116.

Penny, J. (2017) Between coercion and consent: The politics of 'cooperative governance' at a time of 'austerity localism' in London, *Urban Geography*, 38(9), 1352–73.

Pierre, J. and Stoker, G. (2002) Toward multi-level governance, in P. Dunleavy, A. Gamble, R. Heffernan, I. Holliday and G. Peele (eds) *Developments in British Politics*, Basingstoke: Palgrave.

Pill, M. (2012) Neighbourhood initiatives in Wales and England: Shifting purposes and changing scales, *People, Place & Policy*, 6(2), 76–89.

Pinkerton, J. and Campbell, J. (2002) Social work and social justice in Northern Ireland: Towards a new occupational space, *The British Journal of Social Work*, 32(6), 723–37.

Plowden, W. (2003) The compact: Attempts to regulate relationships between government and the voluntary sector in England, *Nonprofit and Voluntary Sector Quarterly*, 32(3), 415–32.

Popple, K. and Redmond, M. (2000) Community development and the voluntary sector at the millennium: The implications of the third way in the UK, *Community Development Journal*, 35(4), 391–400.

Powell, F. (2007) *The Politics of Civil Society: Neoliberalism or Social Left?*, Bristol: Policy Press.

Powell, M. (2000) New Labour and the third way in the British welfare state: A new and distinctive approach?, *Critical Social Policy*, 20(1), 39–60.

Putnam, R. (1995) Bowling alone: America's declining social capital, *Journal of Democracy*, 6(1), 65–78.

Putnam, R. (2000) *Bowling Alone: The Collapse and Revival of American Community*, New York: Simon and Schuster.

Raco, M. (2003) Remaking space and securitising space: Urban regeneration and the strategies, tactics and practices of policing in the UK, *Urban Studies*, 40(9), 1869–87.

Raco, M. (2005) Sustainable development, rolled-out neoliberalism and sustainable communities, *Antipode*, 37(2), 324–47.

Raco, M. and Flint, J. (2001) Communities, places and institutional relations: Assessing the role of area-based community representation in local governance, *Political Geography*, 20(5), 585–612.

Rees, J. (2014) Public sector commissioning and the third sector: Old wine in new bottles?, *Public Policy and Administration*, 29(1), 45–63.

Rees, J. and Mullins, D. (2016) The third sector delivering public services: Setting out the terrain, in J. Rees and D. Mullins (eds) *The Third Sector Delivering Public Services*, Bristol: Policy Press, pp 1–18.

Rhodes, R.A.W. (1996) The new governance: Governing without government, *Political Studies*, 44(4), 652–66.

Rhodes, R.A.W. (1997) *Understanding Governance: Policy Networks, Governance, Reflexivity and Accountability*, Buckingham: Open University Press.

Robson, M.H. (1989) Independent schools and tax policy under Mrs Thatcher, *Journal of Education Policy*, 4(2), 149–62.

Rolston, B. (2007) Demobilization and reintegration of ex-combatants: The Irish case in international perspective, *Social & Legal Studies*, 16(2), 259–80.

Schinkel, W. and van Houdt, F. (2010) The double helix of cultural assimilationism and neo-liberalism: Citizenship in contemporary governmentality, *The British Journal of Sociology*, 61(4), 696–715.

Seligman, A.B. (1992) *The Idea of Civil Society*, New York: Free Press.

Selman, P. and Parker, J. (1997) Citizenship, civicness and social capital in Local Agenda 21, *Local Environment*, 2(2), 171–84.

Shirlow, P. and Murtagh, B. (2004) Capacity-building, representation and intracommunity conflict, *Urban Studies*, 41(1), 57–70.

Shirlow, P. and Murtagh, B. (2006) *Belfast: Segregation, Violence and the City*, London: Pluto Press.

Shirlow, P. and Hughes, C. (2015) *A Survey of Conflict-Related Prisoner's Needs*, Belfast: Tar Isteach.

Shirlow, P., Graham, B., McEvoy, K., ÓhAdhmaill, F. and Purvis, D. (2005) *Politically Motivated Former Prisoner Groups: Community Activism and Conflict Transformation*, Belfast: Northern Ireland Community Relations Council.

Siisiäinen, M. (2000) Two concepts of social capital: Bourdieu vs. Putnam, Presentation to the International Conference on 'The Third Sector', Dublin.

Smith, G. (2007) Margaret Thatcher's Christian faith: A case study in political theology, *Journal of Religious Ethics*, 35(2), 233–57.

Smith, M. and Jones, R. (2015) From Big Society to small state: Conservatism and the privatisation of government, *British Politics*, 10(2), 226–48.

Swyngedouw, E. (2009) The antinomies of the postpolitical city: In search of a democratic politics of environmental production, *International Journal of Urban and Regional Research*, 33(3), 601–20.

Taylor, R., Damm, C. and Rees, R. (2016) Navigating a new landscape: The third sector delivering contracted employment services, in J. Rees and D. Mullins (eds) *The Third Sector Delivering Public Services*, Bristol: Policy Press, pp 169–88.

Teasdale, S., Alcock, P. and Smith, G. (2012) Legislating for the Big Society? The case of the Public Services (Social Value) Bill, *Public Money and Management*, 32(3), 201–208.

Thatcher, M. (1977) Speech to Zurich Economic Society, 14 March, https://www.margaretthatcher.org/document/103336

Thatcher, M. (1987) Interview for *Woman's Own*, 31 October, http://www.margaretthatcher.org/document/106689

Torfing, J. (2007) Discursive governance networks in Danish activation policy, in J. Torfing and M. Marcussen (eds) *Democratic Network Governance in Europe*, New York: Palgrave Macmillan, pp 111–29.

Touraine, A. (1995) *Critique of Modernity*, Oxford: Basil Blackwell.

Wagner, A. (2012) 'Third sector' and/or 'civil society': A critical discourse about scholarship relating to intermediate organisations, *Voluntary Sector Review*, 3(3), 299–328.

Welsh, M. (2014) Resilience and responsibility: Governing uncertainty in a complex world, *The Geographical Journal*, 180(1), 15–26.

Westwood, A. (2011) Localism, social capital and the 'Big Society', *Local Economy*, 26(8), 690–701.

Wiggan, J. (2015) Varieties of marketisation in the UK: Examining divergence in activation markets between Great Britain and Northern Ireland 2008–2014, *Policy Studies*, 36(2), 115–32.

Wilkins, A. (2018) Neoliberalism, citizenship and education: A policy discourse analysis, in A. Peterson, G. Stahl and H. Soong (eds) *The Palgrave Handbook of Citizenship and Education*, Basingstoke: Palgrave Macmillan.

Williamson, A., Scott, D. and Halfpenny, P. (2000) Rebuilding civil society in Northern Ireland: The community and voluntary sector's contribution to the European Union's Peace and Reconciliation District Partnership Programme, *Policy and Politics*, 28(1), 49–66.

Wunsch, N. (2018) *EU Enlargement and Civil Society in the Western Balkans: From Mobilisation to Empowerment*, Basingstoke: Palgrave Macmillan.

Zihnioğlu, Ö. (2013) The 'civil society policy' of the European Union for promoting democracy in Turkey: Golden goose or dead duck?, *Southeast European and Black Sea Studies*, 13(3), 381–400.

Index